BRITT'S
KATY, TX

Military History WW2

'SS AIRBORNE unit'

2008   118 pp.

SS-Fallschirmjäger-Bataillon 500/600

SS

Fallschirmjäger

Bataillon

500/600

Budapest – Leskovac – Drvar – Kaunas
– Raseinen – Malmedy – Schwedt –
Zehden – Prenzlau

Rolf Michaelis

Schiffer Military History
Atglen, PA

Book translation by Christine Wisowaty

Book Design by Ian Robertson.

Copyright © 2008 by Schiffer Publishing.
Library of Congress Control Number: 2007941542

Printed in China.
ISBN: 978-0-7643-2944-9

This book was originally published in German under the title
SS-Fallschirmjäger-Bataillon 500/600 by Michaelis-Verlag

We are interested in hearing from authors with book ideas on related topics.

Published by Schiffer Publishing Ltd.
4880 Lower Valley Road
Atglen, PA 19310
Phone: (610) 593-1777
FAX: (610) 593-2002
E-mail: Info@schifferbooks.com.
Visit our web site at: www.schifferbooks.com
Please write for a free catalog.
This book may be purchased from the publisher.
Please include $3.95 postage.
Try your bookstore first.

In Europe, Schiffer books are distributed by:
Bushwood Books
6 Marksbury Avenue
Kew Gardens
Surrey TW9 4JF, England
Phone: 44 (0) 20 8392-8585
FAX: 44 (0) 20 8392-9876
E-mail: Info@bushwoodbooks.co.uk.
Visit our website at: www.bushwoodbooks.co.uk
Free postage in the UK. Europe: air mail at cost.
Try your bookstore first.

Contents

Foreword

Interestingly enough, in the nearly 60 years after the end of World War II there was no extensive history published on the *SS-Fallschirmjäger-Bataillon*. This is astounding, as the *Sonderbataillon* took part in numerous, exceptional missions and difficult, costly battles.

In this book it will be attempted to account for this circumstance. Not only will the missions in the Balkans and on the East and West Fronts be presented, but also their— partly political—background.

This publication cannot reflect the immeasurable suffering that the six-year war brought to the people. It cannot describe the inconceivable atrocities of partisan combat in the Balkans, and it cannot demonstrate the physical and psychological stresses of the soldiers and of the civilian population that are associated with war!

For the creation of this work, state and private archives were utilized: However, due to the lack of information there cannot be a complete documentation. I thank everyone who selflessly supported this work, and remain open to additions and corrections!

Berlin, October 2004
Rolf Michaelis

Introduction

Inspired by the newly formed Soviet *Fallschirmtruppe*, which in autumn 1935 held off a maneuver with approximately 2,500 soldiers, the formation of *Fallschirmeinheiten* in Germany began in summer 1936. The *Landespolizeigruppe* "General Göring," initially called *Polizei-Abteilung* "*Wecke*" z. B. V.—which was formed by the decree from February 23, 1933, from the Prussian *Landespolizei*, and was also transferred to the *Luftwaffe* in September 1935—formed the basis. Initially intended primarily for the protection of the headquarters of the *Oberbefehlshaber* of the *Luftwaffe,* as well as for the protocolar service in Berlin, a *Fallschirm-Jäger-Bataillon* was formed in the *Luftwaffen-Regiment* "General Göring."

In May 1936 the training of the future paratroopers in the *I./Regiment* "General Göring" began at the Stendal air base. In autumn of the same year the army established a *Fallschirm-Infanterie-Kompanie* within the framework of the *Infanterie-Lehr-Regiment*. This led to plans, also for the *Reichsführer-SS* Heinrich Himmler, to form a *Fallschirmeinheit* within the framework of the *SS-Verfügungstruppe*. This began in the summer of 1937 when approximately 30 *Führeranwärter*, mostly from the *SS-Standarte* "Germania," initially completed paratrooper training with the *I./Regiment* "General Göring" in Stendal.

At the end of 1937 the renaming of the *I./Regiment* "General Göring" to the *IV. (Fallschirm-Schützen)/Regiment* "General Göring" in the *Luftwaffe* followed. While on March 15, 1938, the army was able to enlarge its *Fallschirm-Infanterie-Kompanie* to a *Fallschirm-Infanterie-Bataillon*, Himmler's plan was shelved, presumably by Göring's intervention.

On March 31, 1938, the *IV. (Fallschirm-Schützen) Bataillon* was detached from the *Regiment* "General Göring" and renamed to *I./Fallschirmjäger-Regiment* 1. The *II. Bataillon* of the newly formed *Luftwaffen-Fallschirm-Jäger-Regiment* 1 replaced the previous *Fallschirm-Infanterie-Bataillon* of the army with the decree from December 30, 1938.

Not until May 28, 1941, did the army form a *Fallschirmjäger-Kompanie* within the framework of the *Lehr-Regiment* "Brandenburg" z. b. V. 800, assigned as *Kommandotruppe* of the OKW/*Abwehr*. Just three years later, on March 11, 1944, this *Kompanie* was enlarged to *Fallschirmjäger-Bataillon* "Brandenburg" in Stendal for the occupation of Hungary.

After the failure of the *Luftwaffen-Felddivisionen*, as of 1942 and until the end of the war, numerous *Fallschirmjäger-Regimenter* and *-Divisionen* were formed, and in summer 1944 in the west a *Fallschirm-Armeeoberkommando*, whose members, however, hardly received any jumping training.

The Formation of the
SS-Fallschirmjäger-Bataillon

Due to the enormous loss of life, the tragedy of Stalingrad, as well as the foreseeable end of the *Heeresgruppe* "Afrika," led to numerous ad hoc proposals from German civilian and military offices to bring new forces to the struggling Front. As a result, the idea had developed in the *SS-Führungshauptamt*, in addition to access to foreign "volunteers," up to this point labeled as unworthy to serve, such as, for example, Croatians (Bosnians), Latvians, or Ukrainians, to again lead the prisoners of the central penal camp of the SS and *Polizei* in Danzig-Matzkau into combat missions.

This concept was not fundamentally new. The duration of the war had also led to numerous offenses and crimes against military criminal law or general criminal laws in the *Waffen-SS* that could not be avenged by disciplinary means.

In the latter case, the disciplinary superior from the *Kompanieführer* on upwards imposed disciplinary punishment[1] for violations against the military discipline. Such violations could have been:

- not immediately getting up at reveille
- arriving late for duty
- arriving in improper or sloppy attire for service (for example, unclean shoes), disheveled or improper attire for going out, unauthorized casual clothing.
- Poor behavior with superiors, comrades or in public
- Incurring debts, gambling for money, drunkenness, lying to a superior
- Speaking on duty without permission
- Non-execution of an order received

In contrast, the court martial dealt with criminal acts that would not be avenged by disciplinary means. They were, for example:

- cowardice in the face of the enemy
- desertion
- plundering

---

1   In addition to lesser disciplinary punishments, such as a reprimands, carrying out duties out of the usual way of things (for example, punishment drills, guard duty as punishment, or reporting in a certain attire – socalled "Maskenball"), light arrest for four weeks, aggravated arrest for three weeks, and strict arrest for 10 days could be declared. Furthermore, other ranks could be reduced by one or several ranks.

- Guard misconduct
- Rape
- Misuse of authority in service
- Absence without leave, violation of vacation over seven days
- Disobedient in difficult circumstances
- Theft, in particular, theft of comrades
- Betrayal of military secrets

Here, the stated terms of imprisonment for members of the *Waffen-SS* and *Polizei* were carried out in the SS and *Polizei* penal camp, which was erected after the Poland campaign in Danzig-Matzkau—death penalty by firing squad.

Himmler, who, in his outward decorations, which were based on incorruptible virtues, did not see any place for such members, came upon the idea in 1941 to form a socalled "verlorener Haufen,"[2] "in which convicts are given the opportunity to fall in the field to avoid carrying out their sentence."[3] Here, it was clear that there was no place in the *Waffen-SS* and Polizei for such men.

While the plans for the official formation of a "verlorener Haufen" dragged on for months by the order of the *Reichsführer-SS*, the former inspector of the concentration camps and, at the time, *Kommandeur* of the *SS-Totenkopf-Division*, SS-*Gruppenführer* and *Generalleutnant* of the *Waffen-SS* Eicke, formed a similar *Sondereinheit* in spring 1942 in the Kessel von Demjansk. Court martialed convicts, who could not be brought to Danzig-Matzkau due to the circumstances, received the order to hold a strategically useless section of the Front that was always heavily attacked from three sides. The loss of the soldiers amounted to practically 100%.

Approximately one and a half years after the first correspondence, questions and different opinions between the single SS offices were clarified, such that the *Hauptamt SS-Gericht* became active, and in spring 1943 examined the qualifications of approximately 600 prisoners of the penal camp of the SS and *Polizei* Danzig-Motzkau for Front probation. From the "verlorener Haufen" of 1941, with regard to the war situation, they were dispatched in the meantime, moreso the men were able to be rehabilitated in the troop or a *Sondereinheit*

---

2   The expression "verlorener Haufen" stems from the early time of the mercenary and lansquenet of the Middle Ages. Here it deals with formations that were established above all from sentenced offenders of all social classes, as well as adventurers who hoped to attain gold and fame more quickly. They were deployed in especially costly combat, during which they often went "verloren" (missing). Surviving offenders could be rehabilitated.
3   Letter from the head of the *Hauptamt SS-Gericht*, *SS-Sturmbannführer* Burmeister, to *SS-Richter* with *Reichsführer-SS*, *SS-Obersturmbannführer* Bender, Tgb. Nr. 110/42 secret from June 26, 1942.

of the *Waffen-SS*.[4] If this *"opportunity for probation"* during a war situation also seems opportunistic today, the desire to pay off the remainder of the sentence in a special mission was certainly great. The treatment of the prisoners in the penal institution was normally rough. The *Kommandant* of the penal camp of the SS and *Polizei*, *SS-Obersturmbannführer* Lücke, mentioned this form of *"regulations purely specific to the camp"* in a letter regarding the selection of future *Bewährungsschützen* in February 1943[5]:

> *"The selection and assignment take place first and foremost according to the idea that I have formed on the basis of personal knowledge and study of the files on character reliability of those named during a potential mission. Under these circumstances judgment obviously differs slightly, which the men here in camp learn, because here in the camp during assessment, offenses against prohibitions, such as the smoking ban, are judged leadership wise, which I did not consider in this particular case. I cannot judge a man temperamentally less worthy for multiple violations of the smoking ban or otherwise regulations purely specific to the camp. I have placed much value on assessment and leadership in the troop, especially during missions, and when this assessment was not significant, only then did I decide on the inclusion in the list when the person concerned had proven an inner change through his leadership."*

If it is not clarified to this point in which formation and mission the prisoner should fight, the formation of an independent *SS-Fallschirm-Banden-Jäger-Bataillon* emerged in summer 1943.

On August 9, 1943, the *SS-Richter* with the *Reichsführer-SS* informed the *Hauptamt SS-Gericht* that only a fraction of the selected convicts were fit for a *Fallschirm-Jäger-Bataillon*. However, Himmler adhered to his instructions, to initially detail all available offenders to the formation of this *Bataillon*. Just four weeks later, on September 6, 1943, the SS-*Führungshauptamt* announced the formation of a *SS-Fallschirm-Jäger-Bataillon* for the mission in partisan combat with the *Bewährungs-Abteilung* of the *Waffen-SS* in Chlum (protectorate). Under the command of *SS-Sturmbannführer* Gilhofer[6] the unit was to be organized as follows:

---

4   Letter from the *Hauptamt SS-Gericht* to the *SS-Richter* with the *Reichsführer-SS*, Tgb. Nr. 312/43 secret from February 5, 1943.
5   Letter of the *Kommandant* of the penal camp of the SS and *Polizei* to the *SS-Richter* with the *Reichsführer-SS* from February 10, 1943.
6   For the biography see Appendix 5

Bataillonsstab with
    Nachrichtenstaffel
    Kradmeldestaffel
    Meldestaffel
    Abteilung III (Jurisdiction)
    Versorgungskompanie with
        Versorgungsstaffel
        medical and dental *Staffel*
        Kraftfahr-Instandsetzungsstaffel
3 *Jägerkompanien*
1 heavy *Kompanie* with
    Heavy *Granatwerfer-Zug* (4 Werfer 8.14cm)
    Leichtgeschütz-Zug (4 Fallschirm-LG 7.5cm)
    Flammenwerfer-Zug
    Heavy *MG-Zug*

Initially most official positions were occupied by former *SS-Führer* and *Unterführer* who were demoted; for external recognition:

Gruppenführer	1 Balken
Zugführer	2 Balken
Kompanieführer	3 Balken

was worn on their sleeves. *Ersatztruppenteil* for the *Rahmenpersonal* not previously convicted formed the *SS-Panzer-Grenadier-Ausbildungs-* and *Ersatz-Bataillon* 35. For the *Bewährungsschützen*, the *Bewährungsabteilung* of the *Waffen-SS* Chlum (SS military training area "Bohmen") represented the appropriate *Ersatztruppenteil*.

After intensive *Infanterie* training in Chlum, the *SS-Fallschirm-Jäger-Bataillon* was transferred to Serbia in December 1943 for further training and an assignment in the "Bandenbekämpfung." Stationed in Maturuschka-Banja, jumping training at the *Fallschirmspringerschule* III of the *Luftwaffe* followed in Kraljewo. Furthermore, on February 8, 1944, a *Feldausbildungskompanie* (field post number 28 933) was formed here under the leadership of *SS-Hauptsturmführer* Leifheit.[7] After high physical demands were originally placed on paratroopers, this was reduced during the course of the war, and exhibited a great tolerance in particular among the *SS-Bewährungsschützen*. The ordinance gazette of the *Waffen-SS* documented at the beginning of 1944 that, among others, also *"those half-blind and denture wearers"* were also fit (sic!):

"1. Fallschirmschützen fitness required unrestricted use of infantry duty.
The precondition is active service fitness (k.v.) according to the "medical instructions for the assessment of war serviceability during war examinations" from August 12, 1942, with

---

7   The *Kompanie* was initially transferred to Papá/Hungary in June 1944, and in September 1944 to Iglau. Finally it was incorporated in Neustrelitz as 1. *Kompanie* for the replenishment of the *SS-Fallschirm-Jäger-Bataillon* 600 in November 1944.

regard to the ordered reform of the handling of these instructions – according to the decree from January 21, 1944, from the head of the SS-Führungshauptamt Az: 49a – hö.
The psychological state that is expressed in the voluntary reporting to the Fallschirmtruppe is to be valued as top priority. It compensates for physical faults of a minor degree.
2. Beyond the concept "k. v." the following demands are to be placed on the Fallschirmschützen:

a)   *Height from 160 to 185 cm*

b)   *The age for* Unterführer *and* Mannschaften *is set for up until the completed 30th year of life, for* Führer *until the completed 35th year of life, furthermore, in special circumstances beyond that.*

c)   *With injuries to the spine, an in depth examination is required. Injury to the vertebrae makes one unfit.*

d)   *Overexcitability of the equilibrium apparatus (airsickness) makes one unfit*

e)   *After a concussion or cerebral contusion an extensive examination, perhaps by a specialist, is required*

f)   *In each eye, without glasses, there should be at least half of the visual function present that is fully corrected by glasses.*

g)   *Regarding removable dentures, chewing normal food without dentures may not be fundamentally affected.*

h)   *Stuttering makes one unfit*

i)   *Hernia makes one unfit*

j)   *Wearing special parachuting clothing may not be impaired by vein dilation on the spermatic cord, testicular swelling, or deflections of the thorax.*

3. The issue of a flier-medical report is not necessary."

While the *Bewährungsschützen* of the penal camp were to form the *Schützen-Kompanien* of the *SS-Fallschirmjäger-Bataillon*, the previously convicted members of the *Waffen-SS* were not enlisted as *Rahmenpersonal* in circulars. A former member recalls:

"At the beginning of October 1943 I reported to the Fallschirmjäger of the Waffen-SS, which was to be newly formed, in Salzburg with three comrades and SS-Obersturmführer Fischer from the SS-Gebirgsjäger-Ausbildungs- and Ersatz-Bataillon 6 from Hallein.
We were four Unterscharführer, *who wanted to go back to our old units in the* Division *"Reich" because adventure was lacking. After an entire Bataillon of Mussulmans came for training in summer – despite some interpreters one didn't understand the other – we were fed up.*

One day a writer from the Bataillon *orderly room said that an order came in from the very top, according to which men who would voluntarily report to the* Fallschirmjäger *may not be kept back.*

On the list where one could report, oddly only internal ranks were listed. There were no Frontunterführer *or* Führer *indicated. Because none of us had any desire to play forager or* Waffenkämmerer, *we reported as* Fallschirmwarter *in the hopes to be able to jump.*

On October 7, 1943, we moved off from Hallein, and just three days later we arrived in Chlum in the protectorate.

We reported our arrival to the sarge, SS-Hauptscharführer *Henneck or Henneke, or similar in the* Bataillon *orderly room. He suffered a head injury during combat in Tito's headquarters, and later fell during combat in the area of Kauen in Lithuania.*

*After the sarge took down our particulars he said, pointing his finger at us: '*Fallschirmwart *1., 2., 3., 4.* Kompanie.' *Referring to my objection that I had never before seen a parachute up close – in the hopes that I would be assigned as* Frontunterführer *– the sarge said: 'Take comfort, I also don't know what a chute looks like.'*

Just when we wanted to go, we saw a Kompanie *of soldiers through the window march by the house. However, we weren't able to determine what kind of soldiers they were. They wore only black collar patches without SS runes, no badge displaying rank, and also no decorations on their chest. The entire thing seemed strange to me, and I asked the sarge what kind of soldiers they were. He said that they were the future paratroopers. And the clothing was not due to secrecy, but rather they were all* Bewährungsmänner *from the "verlorener Haufen." I went to* SS-Obersturmführer *Fischer and asked him if he had known. He was likewise flabbergasted when I reported this news. We reported to our* Kommandeur *and wanted to be transferred back to our old units in the Division 'Das Reich.' We arrived in the nick of time. We had just hardly expressed our wish, when the* Kommandeur *kicked us out of his quarters. He said he also didn't do anything wrong, and had to carry out an order, and the same went for us. With this we were dismissed and became* Fallschirmjäger.

We didn't have much to do in Chlum, SS-Obersturmführer *Fischer became Adjutant, and I had to make several business trips for him. There were neither airplanes nor parachutes nor jumping training. Our address read: Seltschan bei Beneschau, Chlum, Groß Knowitz, Böhmen-Mähren.*

In December 1943 we were transferred to Mataruschka-Banja, by Kraljewo. Mataruschka-Banja in German: Marienbad. There hot sulfur springs flow from the earth. The location itself consisted of various hotel-like buildings, a bathhouse, and several other houses. I bathed as much as possible in the warm sulfuric water.

Our Bataillon *was accommodated like a* Kompanie *in the hotels. The* Vorkommando *that was in Mataruschka-Banja several weeks before us already had one dead because of partisans...*

Our trainers at the Fallschirmspringerschule III *Kraljewo were all old, experienced "Hasen," and had already completed several jumping assignments. They were, not as otherwise expected with the* Fallschirmjäger, *fine fellows in every way with whom we had contact very quickly, and with whom we got along well.*

We were divided into groups of 10 men. I was with the Unterführergruppe *from the* Stab, *and had an* Unteroffizier *of the* Luftwaffe *as a trainer. Initially we received a lesson on the nature of the* Fallschirmtruppe, *the form and manner of war. It was explained to us that our greatest advantage was the moment of surprise during the jump into enemy territory. It was explained to us, the faster we jumped out of the plane, the closer the landing of a* Gruppe *was, or rather the* Zug. *If someone hesitated for only a second, at landing it would amount to a distance of 40 to 50 meters between comrades.*

Then we received jumper equipment: jumper helmet – combination in camouflage colors, the jumper shoes, and the RZ 20 parachute. We had to label this chute with our names, because each was responsible for his own chute. We learned the numerous packing procedures and grips to set and fold the 55 m² large silk, so that during the jump it would in fact open and bring us safely to the ground. Many a happy-go-lucky sort of person among us, who in his life had not taken everything so seriously, had suddenly become a meticulous soldier while packing his chute. We practiced getting out of the aircraft on an old wrecked "Tanke Ju 52," we learned the role forwards and backwards from a standing position and from flight. In addition, we were, hanging in the straps, hoisted with a cord approximately 1.5 to 2 meters and, like a swing, set swinging. The trainers had a line in their hands and called out: "40 meters – 30 meters – 10 meters – 10 meters – ready to land!" Then he pulled the line, the cord was released from the strap, and we dropped to the mat lying under us, and had to do a roll forwards or backwards according to the given direction of the wind. Or we had to jump from a 10-meter tower in a belly landing into a safety net that was spread out by the comrades. Another way of becoming familiar with the chute: a Ju 52 without wings was in front of the hangar with the tail end secured to the landing strip. With buckled practice chutes we had to position ourselves behind it, and then the pilot turned on the engine. The wind from the propellers inflated the chute and drove it, with us as an appendage, over the area. While being dragged there we had to open the breast and thigh straps. The chute collapsed upon itself without any trouble...

After three weeks it had come thus far, we were permitted to enter an aircraft, a Ju 52, for the first time. It was the first flight of my life. We had waited a long time for this, and it had finally come to this point. Always 10 men to a plane. This first flight was made without parachutes. It was the socalled orientation flight, and we were to become familiar with the feeling of flying... After this flight the jumping was to really begin.

We were told that each person could refuse a jump three times. After the third refusal he would be transferred back to his former unit. I can't remember, that one person of our Bataillon *would have refused to jump. From the* Kommandeur *to the last man, all had made the six obligatory jumps.*
The first jump was made from an approximately 600-meter altitude with wooden dummies as weapons. Then each time 100 meters less – during the last jump, that was war-like, with all weapons and live munitions, from the air silhouette targets were shot with rifles and submachine guns. We were now fully trained Fallschirmjäger *and ready for duty."*

A former member recalls the relationship between the *Rahmenpersonal* and the *Bewährungsschützen* from the penal camp of the *Waffen-SS* and *Polizei*:

"Regarding the men from Danzig-Matzkau, there was a large spectrum of characters. With many I thought, how could they have been enlisted at all into the Waffen-SS? *Most fit in without a problem, and were happy to have escaped the penal camp. Everything had to happen in a rush – also when the men were detailed to clean-up operations in Danzig. Some did not abandon themselves to hope to be integrated into society again, and the characterization* "verlorener Haufen" *often circulated. They believed that they would be led into a hopeless mission, so they labeled themselves as* ABC-Schützen. *A for soldiers in fatigue duty (*"Arbeitsdienst"*) (clearing debris), B for* Bewahrungsschützen, *and C for* Chlorkalk-Schützen *(Fallen soldiers in graves were often covered with chlorinated lime. When they noticed that the SS members not previously convicted were to go into mission along with them, their opinion changed.)"*

A socalled *B-Schütze (Bewährungsschütze)*—recognizable by the simple black collar patch—in the gray *Luftwaffe* jump smock 1st style.

This *SS-Bewährungs-Schütze* was outfitted with the *Luftwaffe* jump smock 2nd style.

"Dry runs" before the first jump.

Repair...

And packing of the RZ 20 parachutes.

Mission in Southeast Europe

The Partisan Movement in the former Yugoslavia

After the *SS-Fallschirmjäger-Bataillon* found use in the "Bandenbekämpfung" in the former Yugoslavia, the situation at the time is briefly illuminated! Interestingly enough, after approximately one year after the Yugoslavia campaign ended in the spring of 1941 there were greater rebellion movements. Deserted Yugoslavian solders and sections of the unemployed rural population above all had unsettled the regions, so that the unified movement of General Mihailovic,[8] rooted in monarchist, greater Serbian nationalism, emerged. In addition, in autumn 1942 the communist movement emerged, which began in Jaice from the "National Liberation Committee" under Josip Broz "Tito,"[9] and was another factor to be taken seriously.

At the beginning of 1943 the first comprehensive German actions were taken against the partisans. After allied successes in North Africa, the German leadership feared a possible Anglo-American invasion of the Croatian coast. With Operation "Weiß I - III" the *Oberbefehlshaber* "Südost"[10] attempted to silence the partisan movement under Tito that was supported and tolerated by large segments of the population in their core region. Although the operations caused heavy losses to the partisans and drove them off to the Montenegrin border until the end of February 1943, they did not bring about complete success. In May 1943 Operation "Schwarz" was carried out, which was directed at the partisans under Mihailovic in Montenegro. Due to the reaction of the Italian allies (former mare nostro politics) controlling large sections of the Balkans, a sweeping success did not take place.

The discrepancies with Italy increased, and were expressed a few weeks later in Italy's armistice with the Allies. Nevertheless, Mussolini's[11] dismissal came more or less as a surprise to the German leadership. Because German troops were not sufficient in the Balkans to take over the entire area of the Italian formations, the Yugoslavian partisans could occupy, above all, the coastal strip and the islands offshore. The Anglo-American leadership instructed its new ally Italy to maintain single important islands, such as Korfu, for example, in order to maintain a base from there if necessary for an invasion. They feared that Tito and Stalin would prevent the personnel influence of the Western Allies on the Balkans. After German formations had brought most of the islands under their

---

8   Mihailovic belonged to the Yugoslavian exile government in London as Minister of War.

9   For the biography see Appendix 5

10   The *Oberbefehlshaber* of the *Heeresgruppe* "F," *Generalfeldmarschall* Freiherr von Weichs, assumed the function of the *Oberbefehlshaber* "Südost" in personal union as of August 26, 1943.

11   For the biography see Appendix 5

control again in autumn 1943, a significant importance fell to the Lissa (Vis) island. As an offshore island, Lissa formed the main trade center of English support for Tito. From here the weapons, munitions, and other supplies were brought with small transport gliders to the coast, and from there into the mountains to the partisan formations.

The island that was expanded by Tito's partisans to form a proper stronghold was to be occupied as quickly as possible. However, the German lack of forces did not permit an attack until March 1944. In the socalled Operation "Freischütz" sections of the 118. *Jäger-Division*, a *Pionier-Landungs-Bataillon*, the *SS-Fallschirmjäger-Bataillon* as well as forces of the *Marine* and *Luftwaffe* were to be deployed. The attack planned for the time between March 15-20, 1944, was initially deferred due to the developments in Hungary, and finally completely shelved by Hitler on April 23, 1944. The *Luftwaffe* repeatedly bombarded the Adria island, and thus prevented, among others, the erection of an airport.

Excursus: The Occupation of Hungary

In spring 1942 German-Hungarian tensions were already visible. Here it concerned the desire of *Reichsverweser* Admiral von Horthy to leave the war on the German side. The Hungarian government repeatedly disassociated itself from Germany before other countries. The Hungarian endeavor to liberate its divisions from the Eastern Front was also of significant importance!

After Italy's surrender on September 8, 1943, the loyalty to the alliance was again questioned, and the *Wehrmachtführungsstab* worked out plans on how Hungary and Romania's potential break could be prevented. The occupation of both countries (Case "Margarethe I and II") and the appointment of the new German-oriented government were fundamentally contemplated. On December 3, 1943, the head of the *Generalstab* of the *Oberbefehshaber* "Südost," General Foertsch, was ordered to the *Führerhauptquartier* and introduced into the case "Margarethe I"—the occupation of Hungary. Here, it emerged that in Hungary after the occupation a new national government was to be appointed that would bind the country closer to Germany. If necessary, the entire Hungarian *Wehrmacht* was to be disarmed.

The preparation of the necessary German *Truppenverbände* for the occupation led during the then exceedingly tense war situation (among others through the Soviet offensive by Tarnpol) to considerable difficulties. Almost exclusively troops, who found themselves in action or replenishment, were used for this purpose. On February 28, 1944, Hitler ordered to bring the preliminary work to an end.

Under the leadership of the *Stab* z. b. V. Foertsch, four *Kampfgruppen* were to advance concentrically to Budapest and occupy Western Hungary to Theiß:

1.) From the south, under the leadership of the *Generalkommando* XXII. *Gebirgs-Korps*:
- *Kampfgruppe* A from Banat with:
> *Grenadier-Regiment* (mot.) 92
> 4. *Regiment* "Brandenburg"
> *SS-Polizei-Regiment* 5
> *Panzer-Abteilung* 202 (French)
> *Pionier-Bataillon* (mot.) 45
> 1 *Brückenkommando* (mot.)
- *Kampfgruppe* B (*Kdr.* 42. *Jäger-Division*) from the region south of Neusatz with:
> *Kampfgruppe/*42. *Jäger-Division*
- *Kampfgruppe* C (*Kdr.* 8. *SS-Kavallerie-Division*) from the region south of Esseg with:
> *Kampfgruppe/*8. *SS-Kavallerie-Division*
2.) From the southwest, under leadership of the *Generalkommando* LXIX. *Armee-Korps*:
- *Kampfgruppe* A (*Kdr.* 1. *Gebirgs-Division*) from the Virovitica region with:
> *Kampfgruppe/*1. *Gebirgs-Division*
- *Kampfgruppe* B (*Kdr.* 367. *Infanterie-Division*) with:
> *Kampfgruppe/*367. *Infanterie-Division*
> *Kampfgruppe/*18. *SS-Freiw.-Panzer-Grenadier-Div.*, "Horst Wessel"
3.) From the northwest under the leadership of the Gen. Kdo. LVIII. *Reserve-Panzer-Korps* from the region southwest of Vienna with:
> *Panzer-Lehr-Division*
> 16. *SS-Panzer-Grenadier-Division* "Reichsführer-SS"
> I./*SS-Panzer-Regiment* 5
> Heavy *Artillerie-Abteilung* 997
> 1 *Landesschützen-Bataillon*
> 1 *Bau-Pionier-Bataillon*
4.)From the north under the leadership of Gen.Kdo. LXXVII. *Armee-Korps* z. b. V. frm the Neu-Sandez-Neumarkt region:
> *Grenadier-Regiment* 1029 "Großdeutschland"
> *Grenadier-Regiment* 1030 "Feldherrnhalle"
> *Alarm-Regiment* "Brandenburg"
> 1 *Landesschützen-Bataillon*
> 1 *Bau-Pionier-Bataillon*

The *SS-Fallschirmjäger-Bataillon* was to be deployed instead of the *Fallschirm-Jäger-Regiment* 6 of the *Luftwaffe*, which was still not employable. Under the leadership of the *Kommandeur* of the Division "Brandenburg, *Generalmajor* von Pfuhlstein,[12] the *SS-*

---

12   For the biography see Appendix 5

The Occupation of Hungary:
Case "Margarethe"

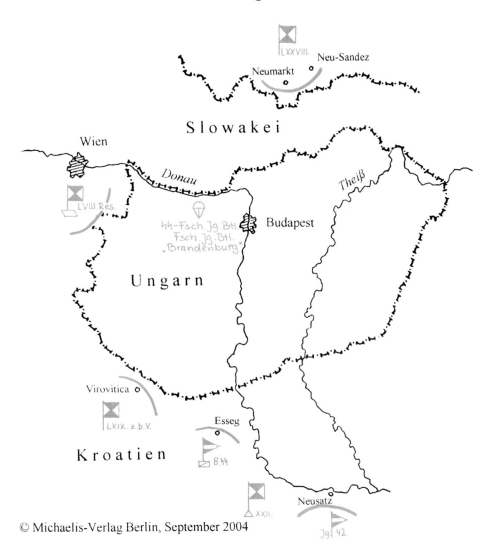

© Michaelis-Verlag Berlin, September 2004

Fallschirmjäger, together with the *Fallschirmjäger* of the Division "Brandenburg" was to occupy all strategic objects in Budapest and prevent a unified leadership of the Hungarian Government and *Wehrmacht*.

The German troop movements in and around Hungary were explained to the obviously concerned Hungarian *Generalstab* with the situation on the Eastern Front. On March 13, 1944, the representing head of the Hungarian *Generalstab* reported to the German *Luftwaffen-Attaché*, *Generalleutnant* Fuetterer, that reports existed, according to which German *Offiziere* in the region of Vienna had remarked that they were appointed for the occupation of Hungary! The head of the *Oberkommando* of the *Wehrmacht* untruthfully stated that these formations were detached to troop trials under the leadership of the *Generalinspekteur* of the *Panzertruppe* Guderian in the Hungarian region.

On the next day, the assignment of the *Gruppe* "von Pfuhlstein" was more closely defined: infantry forces of the Division "Brandenburg" were to announce rail transports independently of each other for March 18, 1944, and then stop and unload the transport trains by self-sabotage around 2200 hours with a distance of 40 km around Budapest. Around 0430 hours the next day the troops were to occupy the castle and citadel within the framework of the Operation "Trojanisches Pferd." The *SS-Fallschirmjäger-Bataillon* together with the *Fallschirmjäger* of the Division "Brandenburg" had to stand by as *Reserve*. The *Reichsführer-SS* instructed the *Kommandeur* of the *SS-Fallschirmjäger-Bataillon* regarding this, to carry out the orders of the *Oberbefehlshaber* "Südost."

Hitler himself invited the Hungarian *Reichsverweser* Admiral von Horthy[13] to Schloß Kleßheim by Salzburg for March 18, 1943, to inform him of the forthcoming occupation, and to demand the removal of the Hungarian government. Without any other alternative, von Horthy explained he was ready to install a new government that was to guarantee *"to continue fighting the war on the German side until the ultimate victory."*

Due to this assurance Hitler refrained from an occupation of the Budapest castle and citadel, as well as the disarmament of the Hungarian *Wehrmacht*. Nevertheless, German troops—also among them the *Fallschirmjäger* of the Division "Brandenburg" and the *Waffen-SS*—occupied the western Hungarian region.

After the new Hungarian government under *Ministerpräsident* Sztójay was announced on March 23, 1944,[14] Hitler dispatched numerous German forces planned as *Besatzungstruppen* to the threatened Carpathian Front. On March 31, 1944, among others,

---

13   For the biography see Appendix 5
14   The Hungarian *Ministerpräsident*—up until this point Miklos von Kállay—was arrested and liberated by U.S. troops from the Dachau concentration camp in 1945.

the order followed for the relocation of the *SS-Sonderbataillon*, renamed three days before to *SS-Fallschirmjäger Bataillon* 500, to Kraljewo for further partisan combat in Croatia and Serbia. Here *Bewährungsschützen*, who had proven unfit for this unit, were ordered back to Chlum. A former member recalls:

"On April 17, 1944, I received the order from the Kommandeur *to bring back approximately 100 men of the* B-Schützen *by rail transport to Chlum, and to give them over to the SS authorities there. It was the men who were unfit either physically or in character for the assignment in the* Fallschirmjäger-Bataillon. *I can remember, for example, that a group of men secretly sold pieces of equipment to the Serbian population or exchanged them for schnapps. By order of* SS-Hauptsturmführer *Dr. Leschinger[15] I had to investigate such a case myself. Here, men from our* Bataillon *had sold boots to the shoemaker master of Kraljewo, and in the second case even pistols to civilians. We were able to find the shoes again at the shoemaker master's, but were unable to find the pistols. Such people were naturally not suitable for the* Bataillon. *In all of the* Kompanien *they are very selective, and whatever was not 100%, came back to Chlum."*

---

15   For the biography see Appendix 5

Last photograph of the *Gruppe* before the first jump.

Line-up in groups.

Ready for the first jump!

Jump from the Ju-52.

Landing.

Operation "*Maibaum*"

After Tito unsuccessfully attempted to attack Serbia from the Montenegrin-Bosnian region in a cohesive major offensive of the I., II., and III. Communist *Partisanen-Korps* at the end of 1943 while suffering heavy losses, in March 1944 he saw the potential for a successful mission by the withdrawal of strong German troops (Operation "*Margarethe*"). On March 22/23, 1944, the III. Communist Corps, with roughly 17,000 partisans coming from the region south of Visegrad over the Lim sector, were able to overrun the primarily Bulgarian *Sicherungstruppen* in the Serbian-Montenegrin-Croatian border zone and advance into the approximately 120 km distant region north of Novipazar. Counterattacks by Ivanjica on March 26, 1944—among others, of a Regiment of the Serbian *Freiwilligen-Korps* and a Regiment of the Russian *Schutzkorps*—led to an evasion of Tito's partisans in the southeastern direction on Raska on the Ibar River.

Because practically no other German troops were available at this time in Serbia, and the low regard for war was evident for the Bulgarian troops, *Generalfeldmarschall* Freiherr von Weichs moved for the return of various troops from Hungary by the *Wehrmachtführungsstab*; the *Grenadier-Regiment* (mot.) 92, the 4. *Regiment* "Brandenburg," the *SS-Polizei-Regiment* 15, as well as the *SS-Fallschirmjäger Bataillon* 500.

The precarious German position in southern Serbia improved somewhat at the beginning of April 1944, as it became evident that Tito also suffered considerable supply problems—on April 6, 1944, the majority of the II. *Partisanen-Korps* focused to the west of Ivanjica, and was itself encircled. In order to help his partisans, on April 23, 1944, Tito ordered the attack of the III. Bosnian *Partisanen-Korps* (16. and 36. Voivodina – as well as 17. east Bosnian Division) to the north over the Drina. The 2. and 5. Communist Divisions, which stood hard-pressed by the German troops by Ivanjica, subsequently attempted to maintain connection to the *Drina-Gruppe* in the northwestern direction in Bosnia. *Generalfeldmarschall* Freiherr von Weichs was aware of this opportunity to annihilate multiple *Partisanen-Divisionen*, and ordered the forces of the Serbian *Freiwilligen-Korps*, as well as the 7. and 13. *Freiwilligen-Gebirgs-Division* to annihilate enemy assemblies in the region between Vlasenica and the Drina. The partisans were to either push against the blocking line formed at the Dirna by the units of the *Militärbefehlshaber* "Südost," or be pursued until their disbandment.

The *Wehrmachtführungsstab* agreed to the plans for Operation "Maibaum," and at the end of April 1944 also secured the release of the *SS-Fallschirmjäger-Bataillon* 500, which advanced from Hungary to Kraljewo on April 5, 1944.

SS-Hauptsturmführer Rybka[16] had taken over the command of the *Bataillon* in the meantime from *SS-Sturmbannführer* Gilhofer.

Operation "Maibaum"
4/26 – 5/10/1944

© Michaelis-Verlag Berlin, September 2004

Under the command of the V. *SS-Freiwilligen-Gebirgs-Korps* (*SS-Obergruppenführer* and *General der Waffen-SS* Phleps) the 13. *SS-Freiwilligen-Gebirgs-Division* "Handschar" positioned their *SS-Freiwilligen-Gebirgs-Jäger-Regiment* 27 in the region south of Zvornik in order to prevent a crossing of the Drina toward the east, following the troops of the *Militärbefehlshaber* "Südost." The *SS-Freiwilligen-Gebirgs-Jäger-Regiment* 28 marched through the Majevica mountains toward Vlasenica. The 7. *SS-Freiwilligen-Gebirgs-Division* "Prinz Eugen" advanced with the *SS-Freiwilligen-Gebirgs-Jäger-Regimenter* 14

---

16   For the biography see Appendix 5

from the Rogatnica region in a northerly direction. The *SS-Freiwilligen-Gebirgs-Jäger-Regiment* 13, as well as the *SS-Aufklärungs-Abteilung* 7, was deployed to the northwest of this area. The *SS-Fallschirmjäger-Bataillon* 500 received the order to go into action on April 27, 1945, and completed the encirclement by Vlasenica. With this four *Partisanen-Divisionen* were encircled.

Although the first *Partisanen-Abteilungen* disbanded, in areas there was heavy combat. For example, at the end of April 1944 in the Sekovici region the partisans succeeded in encircling the I./*SS-Freiwilligen-Gebirgs-Jäger-Regiment* 28. Not until May 1, 1944, could the II. *Bataillon,* as well as sections of its sister Regiment, free the encircled *Kompanien* by force. The *SS-Aufklärungs-Abteilung* 7 had to endure heavy combat—breaking out toward the northwest—with sections of the 17. East Bosnian Division by Kladanj.

On May 10, 1944, Operation "Maibaum" ended. Tito's second attempt to gain a foothold in Serbia was likewise unsuccessful. Thereby, the 2., 5., 16., and 17. *Partisanen-Division*—if not completely annihilated—were brought to the edge of disbandment. For the German side it proved that there was no relying on the Bulgarian allies. On the other hand, the Russian *Schutzkorps*, as well as the Serbian *Freiwilligen-Korps* proved an astounding readiness for action. The quick pulling together of German forces, that not only successfully fought in the resistance of the partisan offensive, but also in the counterattack, is also notable.

The *SS-Fallschirmjäger-Bataillon* 500 transferred back to Kraljewo, and at the end of May 1944 had a strength of over 1,140 men at their command:

Bataillonsstab		267 men
Nachrichtenzug	42 men	
Stabskompanie	66 men	
Kraftfahrzug	30 men	
Abteilung III	7 men	
Fallschirm-Instandsetzungs-Zug	31 men	
Versorgungs-Kompanie	91 men	
3 *Schützen-Kompanien* á	164 men	492 men
1 (heavy) *Kompanie*		200 men
Kompanieführerzug	33 men	
Nachrichtenzug	11 men	
Flammenwerferzug	28 men	
Granatwerferzug (8.14 cm)	34 men	
Heavy *Maschinengewehrzug*	38 men	
Light *Panzerabwehrkanonenzug*	56 men	
1 *Feldausbildungs-Kompanie*		181 men

Operation "*Rösselsprung*"

After the partisan war equaled a battle against a hydra, at the beginning of 1944 the German leadership planned a strike to its heart—an attack on Tito's headquarters in Drvar.[17] The *Wehrmachtführungsstab* made a proposal to the *Oberbefehlshaber* "Südost" regarding this, which was finally realized under the leadership of the 2. *Panzer-Armee*. The 2. *Panzer-Armee* at this point in time was organized in:

> XXI. *Gebirgs-Korps* with
>> 297. *Infanterie-Division*
>> 181. *Infanterie-Division*
> V. *SS-Freiwilligen-Gebirgs-Korps* with
>> 369. *Infanterie-Division* (Croatian)
>> 118. *Jäger-Division*
>> 7. *SS-Freiwilligen-Gebirgs-Division* "Prinz Eugen"
> XV. *Gebirgs-Korps* with
>> 264. *Infanterie-Division*
>> 373. *Infanterie-Division* (Croatian)
>> 392. *Infanterie-Division* (Croatian)
> *Armee-Korps* "Syrmien" with
>> 13. *Waffen-Gebirgs-Division* of the SS "Handschar"
> LXIX. *Gebirgs-Korps* with
>> 1. *Kosaken-Division*
> Available: Division "Brandenburg"

With Operation "*Rösselsprung*" the approximately 750 km² (sic!) large region of Bugojno - Jajce - Banja Luka - Prijedor - Bihac - Knin was to be pacified within 24 hours, concentrically aiming at Drvar. In Drvar, taking advantage of the moment of surprise, Tito and his *Stab* were to be taken captive in an airborne move.

From the 2. *Panzer-Armee,* large sections of the 7. *SS-Freiwilligen-Gebirgs-Division* "Prinz Eugen," as well as sections of the 373. *Infanterie-Division* (Croatian) were deployed. For the assignment, the *SS-Division* was placed under the command of the unified leadership of the XV. *Gebirgs-Korps*. The *Oberbefehlshaber* "Südost," *Generalfeldmarschall* Freiherr von Weichs, provided from his own operational reserve the *Panzer-Abteilung* 202, the 4. Regiment "Brandenburg," as well as the *Grenadier-Regiment* (mot.) 92. From the *Oberkommando* of the *Wehrmacht*, the *Aufklärungs-Abteilung* of the 1. *Gebirgs-Division* and from *Reichsführer-SS* on May 10, 1944, the *SS-Fallschirmjäger-Bataillon* 500 was released for the forthcoming mission.

---

17   At that time Drvar was a small town with approximately 4,000 inhabitants, and was located on the Banja - Luka railway line—split in a valley gorge that the Unac, a small mountain river, runs through.

Himmler did not until later agree with the assignment, because at this point in time he actually wanted to deploy the *Bataillon* to a *"Partisanenbekämpfung"* operation in Oberkrain.

The 7. *SS-Freiwilligen-Gebirgs-Division* "Prinz Eugen" arrived in the west on the morning of May 25, 1944, from the common line Banja Luka - Mrkonic - Jajce. On the western *"Kesselfront"* from the 373. *Infanterie-Division* (Croatian), the II. And III./ *Infanterie-Regiment* 384, as well as the *Aufklärungs-Abteilung* 373 advanced along the street Knin - Bihac toward the east. Southeast of here the *Aufklärungs-Abteilung* of the 1. *Gebirgs-Division* from Granovo advanced toward Drvar. The *Panzer-Abteilung* 202, as well as the *Grenadier-Regiment* (mot.) 92 arrived coming from the north.

Operation *"Rösselsprung"* 5/25 – 6/4/1944

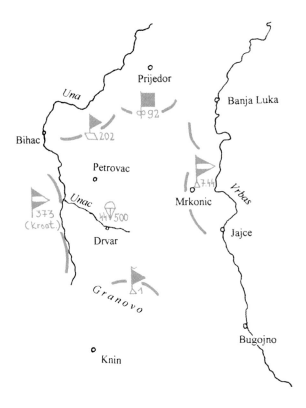

© Michaelis-Verlag Berlin, September 2004

For the air landing in Drvar the *SS-Fallschirmjäger-Bataillon* 500 was alerted on May 20, 1944, in Kraljewo, and shortly thereafter transferred in three transports to the starting airport:

Gruppe 1 (*SS-Untersturmführer* Haselwanter) drove in a motorized march on May 22, 1944, to Belgrad, and from there via railway in the proximity of Groß-Betschkerek.

Gruppe 2 (*SS-Untersturmführer* Witzemann) transferred via railway to Agram roughly 460 km away. The subordinate *Einheit* "Benesch" (Major Benesch) of the Division "Brandenburg" also arrived for the assignment.

Gruppe 3 (*SS-Hauptsturmführer* Obermeier) initially traveled together with the *Gruppe* 2 via railway from Kraljewo toward Agram, however, landed in Nova Gradiska, and on May 24, 1944, advanced in a motorized march (including provisions, weapons, and munitions for all three groups) to the Banja Luka region.

Due to the extreme secrecy of the entire Operation "*Rösselsprung*" the members were not permitted to openly carry their paratrooper helmets, their outfits or their parachutes during these transfer.[18]

From the 1,140 members of the *SS-Fallschirmjäger*-Bataillon 500 approximately 850 participated in Operation "*Rösselsprung*." From this, 654 men in nine *Gruppen* formed the first landing wave, and approximately 200 men the second landing wave.

In the jumping mission the
    Gruppe "Blau" (100 men)
    Gruppe "Grün" (95 men)
    Gruppe "Rot" (85 men)
were to proceed to the citadel and maintain the town together with the other groups until the motorized troops arrived.

Transported in gliders the
    Gruppe "Panther" (110 men) was to conquer the citadel,
    the *Gruppe* "Greifer" (40 men) as well as,
    the *Gruppe* "Beisser" (20 men) was to capture the British military mission,
    the *Gruppe* "Stürmer" (50 men) the Soviet military mission, and
    the *Gruppe* "Brecher" the American military mission.
    the *Gruppe* "Draufgänger" (70 men) were to occupy the radio station.

---

18   The same secrecy was imposed on all troops involved in Operation "*Rösselsprung*." In order to conceal the objective of the mission, the majority of the units did not move into their starting positions until the night before May 25, 1944!

On May 24, 1944, *SS-Hauptsturmführer* Rybka stressed the assignment on the next day:

"The main focus for all sections of the Bataillon is Tito's Oberster Stab. *As soon as it is known exactly where the* Stab *is located, all sections of the Bataillon who land in close proximity to this chief objective must immediately and ruthlessly eliminate above all the* Tito's Oberster Stab. *Important persons should preferably fall into our hands living. Written material of value is to be kept. In the buildings of the* Stab *fires are to be absolutely avoided, so that the men of the intelligence service can come into possession of valuable material."*

Operation *"Rösselsprung"* began during the early morning hours of May 25, 1944, with the bombardment of Drvar. Around 0700 hours the first wave of *SS-Fallschirmjäger* landed, and from three sides attacked Tito's headquarters, located in a rock cave. During the landing there were numerous losses, in addition to fractures the *Fallschirmspringer* received, several transport gliders had crashed during landing: for example, a DFS 230 of the *Gruppe* "Panther," where all occupants lost their lives. The transport gliders of the *Gruppe* "Greifer" was fired on, and had to land 10 km in front of Drvar. In doing so, the *Gruppenführer* fell.

Around 1200 hours approximately 200 *SS-Fallschirmspringer* under the command of *SS-Hauptsturmführer* Obermeier jumped in a second wave. There were again great losses—among others, Obermeier also fell here. After the actual headquarters were empty, the *SS-Männer* secured access to the cave with a log cabin built in front that constituted Tito's actual accommodations. The *Bataillonskommandeur SS-Hauptsturmführer* Rybka was wounded by a hand grenade during the afternoon, and was flown out during the evening with a Fieseler Storch. *Hauptmann* Bentrup took over the command of the *Bataillon*.

Although they possessed information through their own intelligence service of an airborne operation against Drvar, the partisan leadership was obviously surprised. At the time of the attack only several sections of the 3. Brigade of the 6. Proletarian Division, as well as a *Begleit-Bataillon* were situated in Drvar. However, numerous alarmed partisan formations marched out the vicinity—for example, approximately 100 *Offiziersschüler*, who were holding practice or sections of the 1. Brigade.

Hard-pressed because of this, the *SS-Fallschirmjäger*—offered some protection from the wall—had to pull back to the cemetery (approximately 50 x 80 m). Encircled by partisans, the situation soon became precarious due to the poor situation of munitions. German ground attack aircraft and Stukas, which several times intervened in the battles and dropped supplies, were able to provide some relief until nightfall. When on the evening of May 25, 1944, enemy *Granatwerfer* from the surrounding mountains shot at the cemetery, the situation became nearly hopeless—aside from the blank weapon, the men could practically not have been able to counter an enemy assault.

In the meantime, however, after the motorized German forces neared Drvar, the partisans initially pulled back on the morning of May 26, 1944. In doing so, the encircled *SS-Männer* finally succeeded in recovering munitions from a transport glider. The *Luftwaffe* intervened in the combat and dropped additional munitions in supply containers. With the arrival of the soldiers of the 373. *Infanterie-Division* (Croatian) and the 7. *SS-Freiwilligen-Gebirgs-Division* in the course of May 26, 1944, the battles continued to abate. The *SS-Fallschirmjäger-Bataillon* 500 was now under the command of the 373. *Infanterie-Division* (Croatian) under *Generalmajor* Aldrian[19].

The air landing in Drvar, however, did not bring about the desired success; Tito had already succeeded on the first day to hide in the town of Potoci, east of Drvar.[20] The men obtained Tito's newly tailored *Marschall* uniform that was to be later exhibited in Vienna. In the following days Drvar was heavily fought for, as the partisans attempted to conquer back the city. With the arrival of further German troops this could be prevented, as well as begun, to comb through the regions around Drvar. On June 6, 1944, the *Wehrmachtbericht* reported on the preceding battles:

"In Croatia troops of the army and the Waffen-SS *under the command of the* Generaloberst *Rendulic, supported by strong* Kampf- *and* Schlachtfliegerverbände, *attacked the center of Tito's* Bandengruppen *and annihilated them after heavy combat that lasted for days. According to tentative reports the enemy lost 6,240 men. Furthermore, numerous weapons of all kinds and many utilities were obtained.*
In these battles the 7. SS-Gebirgs-Division *'Prinz Eugen' under the command of the* SS-Oberführer *Kumm and the* SS-Fallschirmjäger-Bataillon *500 under the command of* SS-Hauptsturmführer *Rybka had brilliantly proven themselves."*

Although the actual target of Operation "*Rösselsprung*" was not reached with the escape of Tito and his *Stab*, the German newspapers reported a particular success. Among others, SS war reporter Adalbert Callewart wrote a propaganda article with the headline *"The Jump into the Wasps' Nest"*:

---

19   For the biography see Appendix 5
20   On May 27, 1944, a DC 3 brought Tito together with members of the *Oberster Stab*, as well as the various military missions, to Bari. For many months Tito moved into headquarters on the Island Lissa.

"It is still night and dark, as the SS-Fallschirmjäger prepare and climb into the planes. They know their assignment. It sounded very plain and simple from the mouth of the Kommandeur, SS-Hauptsturmführer *Rybka, when he said: 'This time we are attacking the enemy headquarters!' The flight lasts more than two hours. Ten minutes before seven. The target is drawing near, the Jus skillfully fly through two high mountain ridges in a low-altitude flight. The Stukas pull above the transport planes and the ground attack aircraft into the blue aether. There is Drvar! 'Get ready!' the command rings out. The men automatically stand up.*

Hell is broken loose over the small city. Between the detonation clouds of the resistance the Stukas and the ground attack aircraft plunge, the armament rattles, the bombs dully rumble. The great moment has arrived. The horn sounds in the Jus, the sign to jump – and the men jump. The feeling of apprehension has left them. It only lasts seconds, then they all hang in the air and land in the nest of the bandits.

The surprise is complete. Before the bandits can think, the SS-Fallschirmjäger *attack. As they storm forward, the gliders plunge downward and a new* Kampfgruppe *lands. The* SS-Männer *attack. Wherever the bandits want to settle – they are no match for the wild storm of the* SS-Fallschirmjäger. *A* Flakbatterie, *weapons of all kinds, mass quantities of munitions, supply arsenal, secret orders, documents, radios, many captives fell into the hands of the bold* SS-Fallschirmjäger. *The wasps' nest has burnt out.*

At the onset of dusk the bandits advance again. They approach from all sides. But the SS-Fallschirmjäger *have prepared for defense for the night. The bullets whistle from every direction over the heads of the* Fallschirmjäger, *the* Granatwerfer *size up the entire area. The attack is retaliated in fierce fighting.*

It is night, dark night. Nothing can be seen of the desolate mountain ridges that surround the valleys any longer. Some times everything is calm and no shots interrupt the silence. Suddenly the machine guns rattle from all sides and from every corner, and the impact of heavy grenades stir up the defender's position. Reports go from man to man; the radio station is destroyed! Bull's eye! All connections are broken off!

The Kommandeur, SS-Hauptsturmführer *Rybka, is severely wounded. For a moment defeat prevails, then the men swear: 'Now, harder than ever!' However hopeless the situation may seem, and what it will cost, they maintain their position. Between the fighting comrades lie the slightly wounded, who fill the magazine for the submachine guns and prepare the munitions belt for the machine guns. The bandits attack twenty times, and twenty times they are fought off.*

In the east the day dawns. With the first rays of sun the Stukas and the Schlachtflieger *arrive again. A deafening drone hangs over the valley and echoes a thousand times from all mountain ridges. They throw their bombs at the bandits and bombard them with their armaments. Transport aircraft arrive and drop munitions.*

The Fallschirmjäger *charge again and chase back the enemy. When the sun reaches its high point, battle sound comes from a mountain crest. The first* Entlastungstruppen *are there. The* Fallschirmjäger *attack again and force their way. The ring is broken.*
In the blazing sun the Fallschirmjäger *sink down, exhausted, and with a relieved: 'We did it!' they give in to their well-deserved rest."*

A former member, who was dropped in the first landing wave as *Fallschirmspringer* recalls:

"I drove with the Gruppe *'Witzemann' to Agram and was accommodated in a school near the airport. No one was permitted to leave the school or make any contact. None of us, except Witzemann, knew what assignment was before us. We spent one night in the school and were awoken very early, around 0400 or 0500 hours, and the entire* Kompanie *had to gather in a schoolroom. Here we first learned from our* Kompaniechef *which mission was flown. From two-tone glasses we could clearly see the aerial photographs of Drvar. On the aerial photographs we saw lines and drawn in points and each group and each Zug was precisely split up over the landing points, direction of attack, etc. While the* Schützen-Kompanien *jumped with chutes, primarily the 4. Kompanie was dropped for the most part with transport gliders. For the circumstances then, the aerial photographs were very good...*
Tito was mentioned separately and he was to be taken captive either alive or dead under all circumstances. In order to recognize him a photograph of him was shown in his Marschall uniform in a card format. This picture was passed around, but it suddenly disappeared. Witzemann did not receive the picture back. We found it later in Drvar with a fallen soldier of our Kompanie.
The dive-bomber was an outstanding glider in which ten men and the pilot had a seat. The entire fuselage and the wings consisted of light aluminum alloy tube, covered with canvas and camouflage paint. Instead of wheels, under the fuselage a type of sled runner made of wide wood, around which barbed wire was simply wrapped, in order to shorten the land area and to brake. Furthermore, shortly before landing ,on the tail end a braking parachute was cast, which strongly decelerated the steep downward flight. The men sat closely behind one another on a board that was fixed in the middle of the glider and had to push forward with all their power during landing. The advantage as opposed to the parachute landing was that the entire Gruppe *came in closed formation out of the glider and could immediately proceed to the attack. The paratroopers had to gather after landing in order to become a closed group again. If the glider was broken, that was also not bad, after combat operation the pilot simply dismantled the instrument panel and left the aircraft lying there.*

During the battles in Drvar, suddenly two Nietenpanzer, *Italian origin – simply taken away from the Italians by the partisans – arrived. Several called for the flamethrowers, but as these wanted to prepare for combat, it became apparent that during landing they were damaged and obsolete. Subsequently,* SS-Oberscharführer *Hummel tore his camouflage combination from his body, ran toward the last tank, jumped up and held the clothing in front of the observation slit so that they driver would not see anything. However, he positioned the tank across the street and jerked back and forth against the house walls and shook off Hummel. Afterwards a man from the tank crew opened the hatch and shot at the man laying on the ground. A graze to the head was the memento of this event. The tanks quickly cleared off and we never saw them again.*

After two days of hard and costly combat the Division 'Prinz Euge' was able to fight their way through to us and free us from a situation that was slowly becoming hopeless. After our vehicles arrived I received the assignment to bring approximately 50-60 captured partisans to the next town, Petrovac and to hand them over to the Croatian units there who were fighting on the German side. Beforehand, we were attacked several times by American four-engine Bombers and Jabos. Each time it was at least 40 to 50 bombers that unloaded their charges on us...

After several days the Bataillon *also arrived in Petrovac. All movements had to be carried out at night in this region because during the day when we were marching, the Jabos were already there. I assume that the Americans were informed of our movements from the partisans via radio."*

Another former member landed in a transport glider:

"In spring 1944 after graduation from the Führerschule I arrived in Kraljewo (to the SS-Fallschirmjäger-Bataillon) as Junker and provided various services.
Several hours before the Tito-Mission detail took place, I was with the Lastenseglergruppe. SS-Obersturmführer *Schäfer, in whose absence I became deputy, led our* Unterabteilung. *We were to occupy the objective 'Warsaw' (a military mission, Anm. D. Verf.). The* Kampfgruppe *had three transport gliders with approximately 40 men. During the flight, we were transported by Henschel planes, The gliders with Schäfer went 'missing.' We could no longer establish – and it was searched for a long time afterwards – whether it crashed because it was hit or was lost due to other causes. I then had to lead the two remaining transport gliders with approximately 26 men (including the* Flugzeugführer). *During the outbound flight we had quite some luck because a flight of* Jäger *that escorted U.S. bombers (the Ploesti was often attacked then) – did not see us.*

From the good aerial photograph I was able to explain to the Flugzeugführer *where we should land and after that, although already finished, he attempted to come closer to our objective by flying in loops. Nevertheless, we landed approximately five kilometers away, and as a consequence, we few already had approximately 70 prisoners at our objective. At landing we already had to keep the initially gaping and then resisting partisans from our throats with pistols and hand grenades. Those who did not fall surrendered, hence the high number of prisoners. This did not make the path to the actual target any easier, because again and again, with the prisoners running with us, we had to pull new ones from cottages. If they had had more courage to engage us in combat, we would have hardly been able to reach our objective! After landing around 1100 hours, we first reached Drvar around 1300 hours. We occupied a meteorological station that was occupied by Americans and held these cottages until nightfall. We then set off for the cemetery (hedgehog position). Our* Granatwerfer *were set up in front of the cemetery, which plastered the following partisans...*

I set up an MG in front of the Granatwerfer *position and for a long time held the advancing partisans at a proper distance until an* MG-Schütze *fell from a direct hit from a* Granatwerfer– *I got off with a fragment in the neck. Subsequently, we were the last to pull back into the cemetery. The night was illuminated from the tracer ammunition. Early in the morning numerous dead partisans were laying around, whose corpses reeked terribly days later because we did not immediately find them in the area waves.*

During the days after May 26, 1944, we had to survive all kinds of 'combat' with clothes lice! Because at night we had to cover ourselves with seized covers, and these were totally lice-ridden."

A view between Ju-52 and DFS 230.

DFS 230 in tow from Hs 126.

Dropping of the *SS-Fallschirmjäger* from the Ju-52.

Dropping of the first wave
of the SS-Fallschirmjäger over
Drvar.

Dropping of the *SS-Fallschirmjäger.*

Landing of the *SS-Fallschirmjäger* and DFS 230.

Landing of a DFS 230.

Funktrupp and DFS 230 at the Drvar cemetery.

While there was heavy combat in Drvar, by means of airdrop containers, munitions and bandaging material were supplied.

Tito's cave in the mountains west of Drvar.

After the battle...

Replenishing in Laibach

On June 11, 1944, the remaining approximately 200 *SS-Fallschirmjäger* marched out of Operation *"Rösselsprung"* for replenishing in Laibach. Most of the approximately 650 men lost were in base hospitals. The *Feldausbildungs-Kompanie* under *SS-Obersturmführer* Leifheit transferred at the same time with the *Fallschirmspringer-Schule* III to Papá/ Hungary. A former member recalls the march to Laibach:

"During the transfer from Petrovac to Bihat all Kompanien *were on high alert because until we arrived there we were in partisan territory. When the Bataillon made their first stop on a hill shortly before Bihacs and we already saw the lights of Bihac, we thought that we had gotten through the partisan territory quite well. The short rest where we could stretch our legs a little, lasted approximately 15 to 20 minutes. After the short break came the order to get up and start. And in that moment the fire magic started. We received fire first from the right and then also from the left of the street. After the entire Bataillon was completely ready for combat, fire was returned from all infantry weapons, and at the same time the journey continued. Except for a few slightly wounded we had no causalities. The motorized march continued and around mid June we arrived in Laibach."*

Here followed sections of the *SS-Fallschirmjäger-Bataillon* who were not in action in Operation *"Rösselsprung,"* as well as volunteers and *B-Schützen* who arrived later, and who initially had received their jumping training in the *Fallschirmspringerschule* III that transferred to Papá/Hungary. Because discipline with the *Bewährungsschützen* was more difficult to maintain than with soldiers not court martially conspicuous, it was refrained from assigning the *Bataillon* further offenders from the penal camp of the *Waffen-SS*. Thus quickly sank the percentage, of which this group of persons was composed, from approximately 70% initially to roughly 30%.

To bring about a unified management in matters of the assignment and the possibility of probation for offending members of the *Waffen-SS* and *Polizei*, on June 6, 1944, the *SS-Richter* with the *Reichsführer-SS* informed the central office of the *SS-Gericht* that:

to the *SS-Fallschirmjäger-Bataillon* 500
  convicts of the *Waffen-SS* and *Polizei* should come, who were
  sentenced to a prison term
to the *Sonderverband z. B. V.* Friedenthal (*Einheit* Skorzeny[21])
  questionable convicts who possessed a special aptitude and were
  still seen as reliable, and
to the *SS-Sonderregiment* "Dirlewanger"
  All difficult cases and men who were not fit to be *Fallschirmjäger*.[22]

---

21   For the biography see Appendix 5

SS-Hauptsturmführer Siegfried Milius[23] took over the *Bataillon* on June 20, 1944:

"What I discovered in Laibach was an unguided bunch who was given over to me. Except for a few Führer, Unterführer and Mannschaften, the majority did not maintain the rank of Bewährungseinheit. Thus, I realized my first task was to take remedial action and establish some military leadership...."

On June 29, 1944, the *SS-Fallschirmjäger-Bataillon* with a strength of 292 men (15 *Führer*, 81 *Unterführer*, and 196 *Mannschaften*) was dispatched to Gotenhafen/West Prussia.[24] They were to be assigned in an operation against the Alands islands for the blocking of the Gulf of Bothnia with regard to the expected fall of Finland. From there the unit transferred to Rakvere (Wesenberg) in Estonia, and for a short time was under the command of the III. (Germanic) *SS-Panzer-Korps*—however, there were no missions. A former member recalls:

"At the beginning of July 1944 the units were loaded onto trains and via railway traveled across through the Reich to Gotenhafen to the Baltic Sea. I know that we were then brought to Estonia from Gotenhafen via railway transport, but stayed there only a few days and taken back to Lithuania in a rushed transport. Here the Russians had broken through with strong forces by Wilna and Kauen and compromised the Reich's border in East Prussia."

---

22 Compare here: Michaelis, Rolf: *Die SS-Sturmbrigade "Dirlewanger,"* Berlin, 2003
23 For the biography see Appendix 5
24 In the meantime approximately 100 men—mostly convalescents from the base hospitals—reinforced the unit.

Mission in Lithuania

On June 22, 1944, the Red Army with over two million soldiers, 31,00 *Geschützen*, 5,200 tanks, and 6,000 aircraft began their summer offensive "Bagratian" against the Front of the *Heeresgruppe* "Mitte" (3. *Panzer-* 4., 2., and 9. *Armee*). The Soviet 43. *Armee* and the 6. *Garde-Armee* attacked the German IX. *Armee-Korps* (*General der Artillerie* Wuthmann[25]) northwest of Witebsk, and were able to tear a 25 km wide rift between the 3. *Panzer-Armee* (*Heeresgruppe* "Mitte") and the II. *Armee-Korps* (*Generalleutnant* Hasse) of the 16. *Armee* (*Heeresgruppe* "Nord") on July 10, 1944. Because the 3. *Panzer-Armee* was not able to close this breach, the 16. *Armee* formed the *Nahtgruppe* "Kleffel," to which belonged, in addition to the 225. *Infanterie-Division*, among others, also the *SS-Panzer-Aufklärungs-Abteilung* 11.[26] However, these forces did not succeed in restoring the connection to the *Heeresgruppe* "Mitte;" and the encirclement of the *Heersgruppe* "Nord" loomed on the horizon.

Hitler did not allow the recommendation from *Oberbefehlshaber* of the 3. *Panzer-Armee*, *Generaloberst* Reinhardt, to take back the troops behind the Beresina. Thus arose a conflict of interests of the Front *Generale*, to reestablish the connection between the *Heersgruppen* "Nord" and "Mitte," and alternatively to rescue the German troops from annihilation by giving up ground. Hitler's hope to stabilize the Front by stubborn "*Haltebefehl*"—which was successful in Demjansk and Cholm—not only caused the break of the front of the 3. *Panzer-Armee*, but also the entire *Heeresgruppe* "Mitte" within a few days.

The Lithuanian capital Wilna, within the area of the 3. *Panzer-Armee*, was to become such a "breakwater." Appointed by Hitler as a "*Fester Platz*," the Soviet advance to East Prussia was to be impeded here. *Generalmajor* Stahel[27] was appointed *Festungskommandant* on July 7, 1944, and took command of:

> *Grenadier-Regiment* 399
> *Grenadier-Regiment* 1067
> *SS-Polizei-Regiment* 16
> Sections of the *Fallschirmjäger-Regiment* 16
> II./*Artillerie-Regiment* 240
> *Panzerjäger-Abteilung* 256
> *Flak-Abteilung* 296

---

25 For the biography see Appendix 5
26 See: Michaelis, Rolf: Die 11. *SS-Freiwilligen-Panzer-Grenadier-Division "Nordland,"* Berlin 2004
27 For the biography see Appendix 5

The next day there was heavy combat on the outskirts of the city, and on July 9, 1944, the Red Army encircled Wilma—which was to serve as a meeting point for German troops struggling back from the east. On July 11, 1944, Hitler surprisingly quickly authorized the breakout of the stronghold's occupying forces (including the approximately 5,000 wounded) to the west. From the territory west of Kauen an armored *Gruppe* was to encounter the troops.

For this the *SS-Fallschirmjäger-Bataillon* 500—located in the area north of Wesenberg/ Estonia since July 7, 1944—received the order to go into action, and was transferred on July 10, 1944, to Kauen in an air transport. Here, the 3. *Panzer-Armee*, within the framework of the XXVI. *Armee-Korps*, formed the *Angriffsgruppe* "Kauen," which was to establish a connection between the *"Fester Platz"* Wilna and the southern wing of the IX. *Armee-Korps*. The *Angriffsgruppe* consisted of sections:

> *Generalkommando* XXVI. *Armee-Korps*
> *Kampfgruppe/6. Panzer-Division*
> 69. *Infanterie-Division*
> 93. *Infanterie-Division*
> *Fallschirmjäger-Regiment* 16
> *SS-Fallschirmjäger-Bataillon* 500

On July 13, 1944, the *Gruppe* "Kauen" arrived for the relief of the *Gruppe* "Stahel" toward Landwarow. The *SS-Fallschirmjäger-Bataillon* 500 was—under the *Kampfgruppe/6. Panzer-Division*—to take over the infantry securing of the I./*Panzer-Regiment* "Großdeutschland." The *Angriffsgruppe* brought approximately 300 empty vehicles along for the evacuation of the wounded.

The breakthrough of the enemy positions succeeded, and at least 2,000 soldiers of the *"Fester Platz"* Wilna were able to be picked up by the German relief forces by Vievis. During the march back to the German lines, there was once more heavy combat by Zyzmory. The war journal of Pz. AOK 3 reported on the relief of the encircled troops:

"For their relief, sections of the 6. Panzer-Division*, Panther-Abteilung 'GD,' SS-* Fallschirmjäger-Bataillon *500 and 2* Kompanien Fallschirmjäger-Regiment *16 advanced from the territory east of Kauen to the southeast, completely surprising for the enemy. The* Kampfgruppe*, with the foremost tanks that were personally led by the* Oberbefehlshaber*, established a connection with the* Gruppe *'Tolsdorf' after a hard battle against the enemy with Pak and tanks on both sides of the Vievis strait."*

After Soviet formations by Darsuniskis had set out over the Njemen, the *SS-Fallschirmjäger-Bataillon*, within the framework of the *Kampfgruppe/6. Panzer-Division*, was immediately transferred to the south. Here there was—under the *Korpsgruppe* "von

Rothkirch"—heavy combat as of July 15, 1944. The war journal of the 3. *Panzer-Armee* noted on July 19, 1944:

"SS-Fallschirmjäger-Bataillon 500 had the highest losses, fighting strength at the time 220 men."

And on July 22, 1944:

"The counter attack of the SS-Fallschirmjäger-Bataillon 500 for the resolution of an enemy breaks in at least a Regiment strength by Piliuona gradually advanced to hard and costly combat and during the evening had to be called off due to very heavy enemy artillery fire from the eastern short of the Memel, although they succeeded in throwing back two Bataillone of the enemy over the river."

The *SS-Fallschirmjäger-Bataillon* 500 was transferred to Lithuania with a strength of approximately 290 men, and during the relief of Wilna only had an approximate 30-man loss. In the most difficult battles in the Darsuniskis - Piliuona region, however, it

Battles in Lithuania
7/11 - 9/15, 1944

lost approximately 190 men within a few days.[28] The *Oberbefehlshaber* of the 3. *Panzer-Armee, Generaloberst* Reinhardt, on July 26, 1944, reported to the *SS-Führungshauptamt* regarding this:

"The Bataillon *hit very well. In order to maintain the valuable base and with respect to the imminent difficult battles, I strongly request the supply of a 250-300 man replacement, preferably by air to Kauen."*

Only July 29, 1944, when the enemy succeeded in breaking into the HKL to the right and left of the "*Bataillon* sector," were the remaining *SS-Fallschirmjäger* encircled. Under the command of *Kommandeur, SS-Hauptsturmführer* Milius, they were able to push through to their own lines, and again line up into the defensive front. On August 1, 1944, the remainder of the *Bataillon* (approximately 70 men) together with the rest of the *Pionier-Bataillon* 505, the *Pionier-Bataillon* 743, as well as the I./*Fallschirm-Regiment* 21 were transferred to Sakiai for replenishing.[29] Here at least an approximately 100-man relief arrived.

On August 9, 1944, when the Red Army succeeded in piercing through by the northern fighting IX. *Armee-Korps* between 212. and 252. *Infanterie-Division* toward Memel and advancing into Raseinen, the *SS-Fallschirmjäger-Bataillon* 500—practically only the strength of a *Kompanie*—received an immediate order to go into action. Over Jurbarkas - Erzilkas - Paupys - Vidukle the men reached the territory of the 252. *Infanterie-Division,* and during the night before August 10, 1944, intervened in the difficult house-to-house fighting. The *Wehrmachtbericht* reported on the next day:

"North of the Memel the Soviets do not continue their attacks due to losses suffered days ago. In the six-day battle of Raseinen our troops thus achieved a complete resistance success. The Soviets had high losses and during the time from August 4 to 9 lost the supply of tanks of two Panzerkorps.*"*

Together with the *Heereseinheiten,* the *SS-Fallschirmjäger* were able to push the enemy out of the city until August 14, 1944, and capture the dominating height 126.5. The next day the *Wehrmachtbericht* read:

"In Lithuania our Grenadiere, supported by tanks and Sturmgeschützen, threw the Bolshevists from a breach of the last days by Raseinen. 63 enemy tanks and 18 Geschütze were destroyed."

It was additionally reported:

"In the battles in the Raseinen region the troops under the command of the General der Artillerie *Wuthmann have again brilliantly proven themselves by exceptional perseverance and special courage in attack and defense. The formations of the IX.* Armee-Korps *had*

---

28   The losses from July 11 to 25, 1944, amounted to one *Führer,* six *Unterführer,* and 211 *Mannschaften.*
29   With this also ended the present subordination under the 6. *Panzer-Division.*

already distinguished themselves in the heavy resistance combat since June 22. The successes of the leadership and troops had culminated in the six-day battle of Raseinen in which two full, modernly equipped enemy Gard-Panzer-Korps *and at least one* Schützen-Korps *were completely annihilated by 265 enemy tanks mobilized by all tangible forces. Because of the heroic resistance of the troops of this* Korps, *under decisive involvement of the 7.* Panzer-Division *under* Generalmajor *Mauss the intended breach into the territory north of Tilsit was prevented and the precondition for a further successful defense of the East Prussian border was established."*

On August 16, 1944, the SS members transferred to the area south of Raseinen and took position by Sukuriskiai. Here on August 17, 1944, the subordination under the 212. *Infanterie-Division* took place. Two days later the "SS-Bataillon" (strength: 157 men, fighting strength: 90 men), however, was released from subordination, and as *Heeresgruppenreserve* ordered again to the Sakiai (Schaulen) region.

At the end of August 1944 the *SS-Führungshauptamt* planned to supply the *Kompanie*-strong *SS-Fallschirmjäger-Bataillon* 500 to the IV. *SS-Panzer-Korps* combat by Warsaw, which had already fought in the first defensive battle (August 10-30, 1944) partly against two Soviet armies. On August 31, 1944, the second defensive battle began, which lasted until September 22, 1944. The IV. *SS-Panzer-Korps* lost over 3,5000 men in these battles! The *Oberkommando* of the *Heeresgruppe* "Mitte" wrote to the *SS-Führungshauptamt* on September 1, 1944, regarding this:

"The SS-Fallschirmjäger-Bataillon 500 was released from the front and assembled as Heeresgruppenreserve in the Sakiai region.
Currently a transfer from the present assembly area is not feasible with regard to the possibility of a major enemy offensive. The later transfer to the IV. SS-Panzer-Korps *is planned. The date will be announced in a timely manner.*
Considering the development of the situation, it is asked to refrain from requesting the transfer of the Bataillon *outside of the Heeresgruppe area."*

On September 15, 1944, the AOK 4 informed the *I a* of the XXVII. *Armee-Korps* that the *SS-Fallschirmjäger-Bataillon* 500 was supplied to the LV. *Armee-Korps* in a railway transport to Fischborn (East Prussia) on short notice. Here, replenishing (among others, convalescents from base hospitals) took place until September 26, 1944, and the reorganization.

The 1. *Kompanie* was disbanded and divided among the remaining *Kompanien*. The *SS-Fallschirmjäger-Feldausbildungskompanie* was to be called in as the new 1. *Kompanie*. The *Bataillon* initially still consisted of the 2., 3., and 4. *Kompanie* with a total strength of 251 men (fighting strength: 201 men, combat strength: 155 men). In addition, the light infantry weapons the *Bataillon* possessed were 15 light machine guns and an average *Granatwerfer* (8.14 cm).

On September 27, 1944, the *SS-Fallschirmjäger-Bataillon* received the order to immediately transfer to Zichenau/East Prussia. From there, the next day the air transport took place over Brünn to Vienna. The events in summer 1944 not only began happening very quickly on the front, but also politically—in this case, with the Hungarian allies.

Major Witzig from the *Fallschirmjäger-Regiment* 16 of the *Luftwaffe*.

8.14 *Granatwerfer* of the 4. (heavy) *Kompanie*.

SS-Hauptsturmführer Milius.

A *Panzer* IV of the I./Pz. Rgt.
"Großdeutschland" brings wounded *SS-
Fallschirmjäger* to the main dressing station.

Since July 10, 1944, the *SS-Fallschirmjäger* were deployed in Lithuania.

sMG-Truppe goes into position in Lithuania.

Operation *"Panzerfaust"*
The Occupation of Budapest

After the tensions of spring 1944, when the Hungarian *Reichsverweser*—in order to prevent an occupation of Hungary—appointed a new government by pressure from Hitler, in the course of summer 1944 there were further discrepancies. The main reason was the legitimate German assumption that Von Horthy wanted to withdraw from the war on the German side. Although he always denied this, the contact with the Allies did not remain concealed. The first Allied air attacks against Budapest frightened the population, and a negative development of the situation on all fronts increased the long simmering war-weariness. Even though the Hungarian *Wehrmacht* did not possess the morale and the fighting strength of the German troops by far, for the Hungarian military leadership, capitulation—striven for by von Horthy—to the Red Army never came into consideration. Leadership, military, and nation did not form a homogeneous unity in the most different of areas.

Reacting quickly, sections of the 22. *SS-Freiwilligen-Kavallerie-Division* were transferred near Budapest and placed under the command of the III. *Panzer-Korps* arriving here.

At the end of August 1944 von Horthy dismissed von Sztójay for health reasons and appointed *Generaloberst* Lakatos as the new *Ministerpräsident*. After talks on September 11, 1944, in the Hungarian Cabinet of a possible withdrawal of Hungary from the war the members, however, disapproved, and asked the *Reichsverweser* to resign. He not only declined this, but also forced contact to the allies through his son. The right-wing politicians in Hungary planned for the takeover of power—with German assistance.

In mid-October the situation escalated; the SD arrested the son of the *Reichsverweser*— Nikolaus von Horthy—for his actions with the enemy, and not least to put pressure on the *Reichsverweser*. On October 15, 1944, around 1300 hours he announced on the radio that he never pursued imperialistic objectives, and Hungary was forced into the war by Germany. Von Horthy ordered the army to put down their weapons, and requested an armistice with the Allies! Von Horthy was obviously strongly psychologically shattered, because after a conversation with the German ambassador Rahn, he admitted having made a great political mistake. Shortly after 1400 hours a disclaimer followed in the radio, which certainly did not contribute to the alleviation of the situation.

During the evening, a planned action by right opposition with the support of the *Höhere SS* and *Polizeiführer* began. Sections of the 22. *SS-Freiwilligen-Kavallerie-Division*, as well as the heavy *Panzer-Abteilung* 305 were on hand.

The government and the *Reichsverweser* resigned, and a new nationally minded government under Szálasi took over the government business—in close contact with Germany.

Concerning this, in mid-September *SS-Sturmbannführer* Skorzeny received a new special assignment from Hitler.[30] After the anti-German stance of Admiral von Horthy was apparent, Skorzeny was to occupy the Hungarian seat of government—the Budapest castle—and take over the government.

For this purpose, in addition to the *SS-Fallschirmjäger-Bataillon* 500, a *Fallschirmjäger-Bataillon* of the *Luftwaffe*, a motorized *Infanterie-Bataillon* of the *Offizierskriegsschule* Wiener-Neudstadt, as well as the heavy *Panzer-Abteilung* 305 and a *Goliath-Kompanie* was available to him. Skorzeny himself ordered the I./*SS-Jäger-Bataillon* 502 from Friedenthal by Oranienburg to Vienna. Due to the fact that for an air landing only the large drill field in Budapest came into question, which, however, strategically presented a great risk by the enemy position of the Hungarian troops, Skorzeny did without parachute jumps of both *Fallschirmjäger-Bataillone* in his planning.

At the beginning of October 1944 the *SS-Fallschirmjäger* reached the area of the Hungarian capital from their previous accommodations in Deutsch-Wagram. There, Skorzeny arrested the son of Admiral Horthy on October 15, 1944, with the I./*SS-Jäger-Bataillon* 502.

---

30   Skorzeny was already well known in September 1943 after he freed Mussolini at the Gran Sasso.

The next morning Operation *"Panzerfaust"* began. While the 22. *SS-Freiwilligen-Kavallerie-Division* formed an outer blocking belt around the castle and occupied train stations and further important facilities, the *Bataillon* of the *Kriegsschule* Vienna was to advance over the gardens by the southern slope of the castle mountain. Sections of the *Kompanie* of the *SS-Jäger-Bataillon* 502, together with several tanks advanced to the castle from the west. In contrast to the *Fallschirmjäger-Bataillon* of the *Luftwaffe*, which *SS-Sturmbannführer* Skorzeny utilized as Reserve, the main tasks fell to the men of the *SS-Fallschirmjäger-Bataillon* 500. Approximately 30 men—from the chain bridge tunnel—had to penetrate into the corridors under the castle and from below into the War Ministry and the Interior Ministry. Approximately 120 men, together with the remainder of the *Kompanie* of the *SS-Jäger-Bataillon* 502, as well as two *Züge Panther* and the *Goliath-Kompanie*, were to advance over the Wiener Straße and the Wiener Tor to the square in front of the castle in a surprise strike and occupy the supposed center of resistance.

At the first light of dawn around 0600 hours *SS-Sturmbannführer* Skorzeny issued the order for beginning action. He intended to drive over the Wiener Straße to the castle without force of arms; for this purpose he sat in the first vehicle—a military utility vehicle. Four *Panzer* V, the *Goliathkompanie*, as well as approximately 250 *SS-Fallschirmjäger* and *SS-Jäger*, who were on trucks, followed. Without a fight, the convoy reached the castle, the gate of which was blocked by a stone barricade. A Panther collapsed the obstruction and drove into the courtyard of the castle. While at 0630 hours *SS-Sturmbannführer* Skorzeny had already requested the Hungarian *Kommandant* to surrender the castle, on the castle hill—among others at the War Ministry—there were small battles, during which a total of four Germans and three Hungarian soldiers fell.

In Hungary a new government under Szálasi was appointed the next day. The *SS-Fallschirmjäger* were assigned to securing important locations in Budapest, and then transferred to Neustrelitz for replenishment.

Under the command of SS-*Hauptsturmführer*
Milius the SS-*Fallschirmjäger-Bataillon*
participated in Operation "*Panzerfaust*" on
October 16, 1944.

Budapest

Formation of the
SS-Fallschirmjäger-Bataillon 600

In Neustrelitz, numerous administrative tasks could finally be carried out, for which previously there was no time due to constant missions. Here, the rehabilitation of the *Bewährungsschützen* reached a special point. Not least due to the fact that Himmler, for reasons of personal vanity did not want to associate the shortcoming of a "Bewährungsformation" with this unit, the *Bataillon* was renamed from 500 to 600. With effect from October 1, 1944, the *SS-Fallschirmjäger-Bataillon* was no longer a *Bewährungseinheit*.

The meager strength of the Bataillon of only roughly 250 men was to be brought to an authorized strength (approximately 1,000 men) through recruitment in *Ausbildungs-* and *Ersatzeinheiten* of the army in Lower Saxony and Westphalia. In doing so, it was a decisive factor to not burden the existing formations of the *Waffen-SS* by detailing, but rather to supply the Waffen-SS with new "volunteers." In addition, the *SS-Fallschirmjäger-Ausbildungs-Kompanie* (strength: approximately 200 men) was transferred from Iglau to Neustrelitz, and integrated into the *Bataillon* as the new 1. *Kompanie*. The former *Bataillonskommandeur SS-Hauptsturmführer* Milius recalls:

"It must be said that the Kompanien *already looked terribly messy, but the battle-tried soldiers were in no way depressed or less enthusiastic. After the successful Budapest assignment we finally came for rest and replenishment in Neustrelitz in proper barracks. There was vacation as much as possible, and with the help of Skorzeny I could obtain what was missing for a long time through the* Reichsführer.*

In the unit there were men who had proven themselves multiple times in combat missions. One only failed to follow the promises with the deed; that is, the rehabilitation was not followed by complete integration—which would have included a rank." After a short time we were called the SS-Fallschirmjäger-Bataillon 600. *With great joy men, such as the* Kompanieführer Schmiedel, *received the rank of* SS-Obersturmführer. *Even among the* Unterführer and Mannschaften *something was being done. The lawyer assigned to me, SS-Hauptsturmführer Dr. Leschinger, did everything, in fact exemplary, that was to be taken care of as a formality, although everything was not going quickly enough for me or without jurisprudence. For this reason we fought out many quarrels with each other. But we were successful!*

Moreover, Skorzeny made a valuable commitment that helped us extraordinarily during replenishment. SS-Obersturmführer Scheu *received the assignment (and was equipped with the corresponding powers) to recruit volunteers in the* Wehrmacht-Ersatz-Bataillone Genesenden-Kompanien, etc. *He tackled this assignment with such complete success that we could deploy a full battle-tried* Bataillon *with full battle strength. The men of the* Wehrmacht *had settled in with us quickly, and later fought brilliantly like our old SS-Männer."*

From my frequent visits and presentations in Friedenthal (Skorzeny's location), the Bataillon *was equipped weapon-wise with the newest* Sturmgewehr, *MGs, antitank weapons, and explosives. The fleet was brilliantly reconditioned."*

With effect from November 10, 1944, the *SS-Fallschirmjäger-Bataillon* 600 was taken over into the *SS-Jagdverbände*[31] with a strength of 17 *Führer*, 113 *Unterführer*, and 555 *Mannschaften* (Total: 685 men). With this emerged a subordination during action to the *Reichssicherheitskauptamt*! It officially remained under the command of the *SS-Führungshauptamt*. Therefore, *SS-Obersturmbannführer* Skorzeny had at his command in his *SS-Jagdverbände*:

> *SS-Fallschirmjäger-Bataillon* 600
> *SS-Jagdverband* "Nordwest"
> *SS-Jagdverband* "Südwest"
> *SS-Jagdverband* "Südost"
> *SS-Jagdverband* "Ost"
> *SS-Jagdverband* "Mitte" (from the *SS-Jäger-Bataillon* 502)

---

31   In 1943 the *SS-Sonderverband z. b. V.* "Friedenthal" was formed, which was to carry out similar raids like the Division "Brandenburg." From this, at the beginning of 1944, the *SS-Jäger-Bataillon* 502 emerged. In autumn 1944 *SS-Obersturmbannführer* Skorzeny took over the assignments of the Division "Brandenburg," for which numerous units of the Division were placed under his command. Under the *Stab* of the socalled *SS-Jagdverbände*, numerous *SS-Jagdkommandos* finally performed on various theaters of war—mostly behind the front.

Operation "Greif"
The Mission of the Ardennes Offensive

At the end of August 1944 Hitler informed his *Generäle* that he wanted to begin a major offensive on the Western Front during the next weeks that was to present the Allies with a second Dunkirk. The plans became more concrete in September 1944 when the western allies fought in Nijmegen and Arnheim. Hitler intended to pierce through the relatively weakly occupied allied front in the Eifel, to occupy Antwerp, and finally to destroy the approximately 20 enemy divisions north of it. The time of attack was set for late autumn 1944 because the probable hazy weather would relativize the immense enemy air superiority. For this reason two *Panzer-Armeen* were supplied to the *Heeresgruppe* "B" (*Generalfeldmarschall* Model)—unnoticed by Allied reconnaissance and exposure of the remaining fronts. Approximately 200,000 soldiers with 600 tanks and *Sturmgeschütze* were to pierce through the approximately 200 km to Antwerp—a grotesque plan, when one considers that there was hardly fuel or *Luftwaffe* support available, and the attack was to be led through mountainous territory!

On November 10, 1944, the order for action arrived. According to this, the 6. *Panzer-Armee* (*SS-Oberstgruppenführer* and *Generaloberst* of the *Waffen-SS* Dietrich) were to pierce through the enemy front north of the Schnee-Eifel with fast *Panzerverbände*—without consideration of the north flank—cross the Maas, and then advance on the Albert Canal between Maastricht and Antwerp. In contrast, the *Infanterie-Verbände*—along the Weser on both sides of the Eupen and the eastern fortifications of Lüttich—had depended on the 15. *Armee* to protect the north flank.

Preparation for the Ardennes Offensive

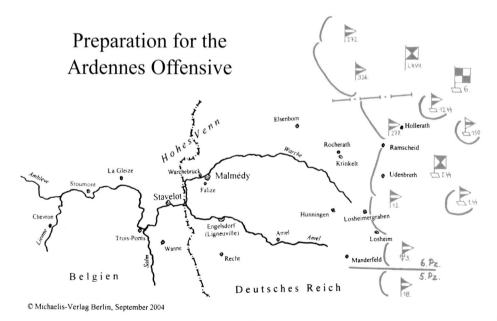

© Michaelis-Verlag Berlin, September 2004

The second supplied *Armee*—the 5. *Panzer-Armee*—located south of the 6. *Panzer-Armee*, was to advance through the enemy HKL in the northern section of Luxemburg, and by using the Straße Bastogne—Naumur advance over the Maas between Amay and Manur. When the situation demanded or presented it, sections were brought forward over Dinant or the Sambre in the Brussels region and west of Antwerp in order to prevent the effects of enemy reserves over the line Antwerp - Brussels - Dinant against the back of the 6. *Panzer-Armee*. Also, the deep southern flank that emerged here was to be disregarded. The quick troops of the 5. *Panzer-Armee*, however, were to ensure a consistently maintained connection to the spearheads of the 6. *Panzer-Armee*. An order that demonstrated how far from reality the German leadership had become.

The 7. *Armee* situated south of the 5. *Panzer-Armee* was to break through the enemy HKL between Echternach and Grevenmacher, and secure the flanks of the 5. *Panzer-Armee*. Finally, along the Maas south of Dinant, on the Smoiss, as well as in the region on both sides of Luxemburg, a defensive front was to be established toward the south.

Because the large bridges over the Maas were extremely important for the successful advance on Antwerp, Hitler intended to prevent the potential destruction of these strategic points by *Kommandotruppen*. Therefore, he assigned *SS-Obersturmbannführer* Skorzeny, already well known from special operations, with the planning of a particular action. Disguised as returning U.S. troops, the German soldiers were to occupy the Mass bridges by Engis, Amay, and Huy, and hold them until the arrival of the German *Panzerverbände*.

At the end of October 1944 Skorzeny began to form the unit, named *Panzer-Brigade* 150 as a code name. Formed at the Grafenwöhr military training area, it was formed in:

I./*Panzer-Brigade* 150 (*Kampfgruppe* "X") – *Oberstleutnant* Wulf
    Fallschirmjäger-Bataillon "Schluckebier"[32] – *Major* Schluckebier
    Panzerspähwagenkompanie
II./*Panzer-Brigade* 150 (*Kampfgruppe* "Y") – *Hauptmann* Scherf with
    Fallschirmjäger-Bataillon "Bading" – *Oberleutnant* Bading
    Panzerkompanie (Sherman-Panzer) – *Oberleutnant* Ernst[33]
III./*Panzer-Brigade* 150 (*Kampfgruppe* "Z") – *SS-Obersturmbannführer* Hardieck
    SS-Kampfgruppe "Leifheit" (I./*SS-Fallschirmjäger-Bataillon* 600)
    SS-Kampfgruppe "Mans" (*SS-Jagdverband* "Mitte")
    Panzerkompanie[34] (5 Panzer V) – *Oberleutnant* Dreier

A former member recalls the first days in Grafenwöhr:

"As the Bataillon, *after heavy combat in Lithuania and a short trip to Hungary in Autumn 1944, stayed in Neustrelitz for replenishment, no one suspected that only a few days later this time of peace would come to an end. Having even hardly arrived in Neustrelitz, we*

---

32   In both *Fallschirmjäger-Bataillonen* "Schluckebier" and "Bading" it concerned the I. and II./*Fallschirmjäger-Regiment z. b. V.* After the Ardennes Offensive both *Bataillone* transferred to Wittstock. They finally formed the *Fallschirmjäger-Regiment* 26 of the 9. *Fallschirmjäger-Division*.

33   On January 22, 1944, Albert Ernst as *Leutnant* and *Zugführer* in the I./heavy *Panzerjäger-Abteilung* 519 received the Knight's Cross.

34   The crew made up the 4./*Panzer-Regiment* 11.

already had to pack again. In a railway transport at the beginning of November we headed southbound over Hof directly into Nordlager to the Grafenwöhr military training area. We carved out a miserable existence in the barracks far away from any civilization. Service and sentry duty alternated regularly. One day we observed that in the large workshops intensive activity prevailed. Arcs of light flickered behind darkened windows and the hammering and knocking could be widely heard. Panzer V (Panther) were expertly transformed into American M10 (Panzerzerstörer). Latrinenpatrolen appeared, and whenever anyone listened: rumors, suspicions, and fears of a special mission in the west made the rounds. The total blocking of the territory around the camp seemed to back up the patrols that appeared again and again."

Because the Ardennes Offensive (Operation "Wacht am Rein") was to begin during the first days of December 1944, only roughly four weeks remained for the formation. While the personnel requirements for the formation of the *Panzer-Brigade* 150 could be secured by detailing the I. and II./*Fallschirmjäger-Regiment* x. b. V. of the *Luftwaffe*, the 4./*Panzer-Regiment* 11, as well as the I./*SS-Jagdverband* "Mitte" and the I./*SS-Fallschirmjäger-Bataillon* 600, the plan to equip the Brigade with American uniforms remained a fiction.

The *Panzer-Kompanie* of the *Kampfgruppe* "Z" received five German Panzer V "Panther," that matched the American *Panzerzerstörer* M 10 through structural changes of the silhouette. In addition to 30 socalled Willy Jeeps, the *Panzer-Brigade* 150 had only four American half-track vehicles and approximately 15 trucks at their disposal. The remainder consisted of German vehicles!

The outfitting of U.S. uniforms could likewise be realized only to a small extent. The OKH did not want to have these confiscated in the prisoner of war camps because it concerned a process against international law. The aspect of "capturing booty"—the fuel for the continuation of the Offensive from the Maas to Antwerp "had to" be obtained—received special importance, also for *SS-Obersturmbannführer* Skorzeny. The majority of the *Panzer-Brigade* 150 had to be outfitted with U.S. uniforms in the course of the first day of the Offensive. The question remained open if this were to happen with the seizure of a clothing storehouse, or the seizure of uniforms from prisoners of war or fallen soldiers. Initially, only the driver or the passenger—whoever commanded sufficient skills in English—wore American uniforms, while the remaining men in the vehicles continued to wear their German uniforms.

The *Kommando* operation for the seizure of various Maas bridges was initially named "Rabenhügel," and later "Greif." The three *Kampfgruppen* of the *Panzer-Brigade* 150 were to overtake the German spearheads after the breach and, disguised as returning U.S. troops, form bridgeheads on both sides of the Maas and hold until the advancement of the *Panzerverbände*. The *Kampfgruppe* "X" was to seize in the area of the advancing 12. *Panzer-Division* "Hitlerjugend" the bridge by Engis, the *Kampfgruppe* "Y" in the region of the 1. *SS-Panzer-Division* "Leibstandarte Adolf Hitler" (*Panzergruppe* "Peiper") the bridge by Amay, and the *Kampfgruppe* "Z"—likewise supplied to the 1. *SS-Panzer-Division* (*Gruppe* "Hansen")—the railway bridge Huy. In addition, small troops in U.S. uniforms and socalled Willy Jeeps were deployed separately in order to cause confusion to the enemy troops.[35]

Due to the lag of the entire deployment, the time of attack was moved initially from December 1, 1944, to the 10th, and finally to December 16, 1944. On December 8, 1944, the transfer of the *Panzer-Brigade* 150 followed (strength: approximately 1,600 men) from the Grafenwöhr military training area to the Wahn military training area by Cologne. During the night of 13 to 14 December 1944 the Brigade marched into the Blankenheim Forest in the assembly area of the I. *SS-Panzer-Korps* (12. *SS-Panzer-Division* "Hitlerjugend" and I. *SS-Panzer-Division* "Leibstandarte Adolf Hitler") at the disposal of the 6. *Panzer-Armee*. On December 15, 1944, this was organized in:

LXVII. *Armee-Korps* with
  272. and 326. *Volks-Grenadier-Division*
I. *SS-Panzer-Korps* with
  277. and 12. *Volks-Grenadier-Division*
  3. *Fallschirmjäger-Division*
  12. *SS-* and I. *SS-Panzer-Division* and *Panzer-Brigade* 150
II. *SS-Panzer-Korps* with
  2. SS- and 9. SS-*Panzer-Division*

On the next day the 277. *Volks-Grenadier-Division* with the *Grenadier-Regiment* 989 from the region of the Westwallbunker, around Hollerath, and the *Grenadier-Regiment* 990 from the region of the Westwallbunker around Udenbreth were to report at Rocherath - Krinkelt and clear the path for the 12. *SS-Panzer-Division*. The *Grenadier-Regiment* 991 assembled behind both *Regimenter* by Ramscheid.

The 12. *Volks-Grenadier-Division* with the *Grenadier-Regiment* 48 had to pierce through the American positions on both sides of Losheim, and the 3. *Fallschirmjäger-Division* in the sector of Berterath - Manderfeld - approaching Hepscheid and Heppenbach - had to make the march through Losheimer Graben possible for the *Kampfgruppen* of the 1. *SS-Panther-Division*.

---

35   The success of the few deployed *Gruppen* varied. They caused chaos for the Americans, who were susceptible to rumors, and a few "genuine" U.S. soldiers were seized temporarily as "fakes." If the German *Kommandotrupps* were taken captive, they were i. d. R. shot!

On December 16, 1944, at 0530 hours in the morning at approximately 100km from Monschau to Echternach, the offensive against the 1ˢᵗ U.S. Army (General Hodges) began. After a 30-minute heavy artillery preparation the 6. *Panzer-Armee* at the Hallscheid - Losheim sector took on the 5ᵗʰ U.S. Corps (General Gerow). The *Korps* of the 5. *Panzer-Armee* (*General der Panzertruppen* von Menteuffel) - LXVI. *Armee-Korps*, LVIII. *Panzer-Korps* and XLVII. *Panzer-Korps* - took the offensive in the region between Manderfeld and Bitburg to the west against the 8ᵗʰ U.S. Corps (General Middleton). In the south of the front the 7. *Armee* (*General der Panzertruppen* Brandenberger) with LXXXV. and LXXX. *Armee-Korps* attacked in the region toward Echternach. A former member recalls the first hours of the Offensive:

"In the night of 15-16 December 1944 I stood on a clearing near the Belgian border. The night was cold, and the shelters on the edge of the meadow were packed with Landser. Everyone was looking for a dry spot sheltered from the wind. Dog tired, we dosed. Around 0300 hours in the morning we were called on. On a forest path stood our Mannschaftstransporter. *We sat up and waited. Guns between our knees, we waited. After a couple hours we first knew what it was about. It was ice cold on the vehicles, the tarp was taken down, and the snowy air swept over the Eifel heights. We couldn't shiver as fast as our teeth were chattering. Everything was numb. Since Grafenwöhr we no longer took off the gear, and we didn't have any winter clothing. Through the thin cloth of the uniforms the cold crept in to the core. The jump smock also did keep anything out.*

Tanks rushed across, a second and a third followed, then there was silence. A strange silence. There stood a fully equipped Panzerarmee *in a narrow area, and that was everything, as far as artillery was concerned, that was sent over to the Americans? The hour was 0530 hours and it remained silent. The drivers had turned off the engines—fuel was low.*

Waiting and again waiting. Finally we got going. With dimmed headlights we proceeded slowly. On the back roads the column rolled into the direction of Losheimer Graben.

We were standing more than we were driving. The merging onto the route of advance did not appear to function. When it became light we finally sat it out. We went uphill by foot over narrow forest paths that were furrowed by tracked vehicles. The first light of day came through the beech forest. With Infanterieeinheiten *of the* Wehrmacht *we marched to the side of the path through the forest.*

Completely loaded with severely wounded, an SPW snaked down the marshy path. Everywhere there was an oppressive silence at the sight of this first visible victim. Going uphill, the wheeled vehicles had difficulty managing to get through. They pulled themselves steeply up to the heights. Despite the cold we soon broke out in a sweat. Mist hung between the trees. No one asked anymore, where we actually were. After hours we arrived to a street, along which a Panzereinheit *had driven on a bordering meadow.*

The Panther had switched off the engines. Snow showers had flown over. We crawled behind the heavy colossus and warmed ourselves on the large exhaust mufflers. Everywhere Gruppen *sat together at secured locations. Several slept....*"

The attack did not move into gear; after the 277. *Volks-Grenadier-Division* did not succeed in piercing through the enemy HKL, the 12. *SS-Panzer-Division* "Hitlerjugend" located behind them received the order for action. But they were also not successful in breaking through; just as little as the 12. *Volks-Grenadier-Division* in the Losheim region. Only the 3. *Fallschirmjäger-Division* could break into enemy positions, and made the fast advance into the territory south of Malmédy[36] - Stavelot possible for the *Panzergruppe* "Peiper"(*Kdr.* Of the *SS-Panzer-Regiment* 1).

With his *Gruppe,* a former member of the *Panzer-Brigade* 150 lost contact to his *Kampfgruppe* and joined to sections of the 12. *SS-Panzer-Division* "Hitlerjugend":

"In order to not be altogether in limbo, we joined with this unit. At least we no longer needed to march on this day. With the Grenadiere *on the back the heavy tanks rumbled on the street. Our tank crew did not look bad, when they caught sight of the unfamiliar steel helmets. But then they were delighted to transport* Fallschirmjäger *as an infantry escort. After a short time driving, the first column of captive Americans came toward us. They anxiously pressed to the roadside while tank after tank rattled by them. From the distance came the sound of combat.*

---

36   Malmédy became a special political issue already in December 1944 when the USA accused Germany of violation of international law with the shooting of 200 U.S. soldiers taken as prisoners of war! On December 17, 1944, the *SS-Panzergruppe* "Peiper" came across a 200 man strong American artillery unit on march four kilometers from Malmédy. Within a few minutes, the American vehicles stood in flames—the majority of the U.S. soldiers surrendered. While the *Kampfgruppe* "Peiper" immediately continued on, approximately eight SS members—of a vehicle left behind due to damage of the treads—took over the guard of the approximately 100 prisoners of war. When three U.S. soldiers attempted to escape into the nearby forest, the German *Panzerkommandant* made use of his firearm. The situation escalated, as now further Americans tried to escape. Now the other German soldiers opened fire. The U.S. troops later found a total of 71 fallen soldiers; however, it could no longer be determined who had fallen during the short battle before being taken captive or just after the capture. On December 20, 1944, the *Soldatensender* Calais reported that by Malmédy 200 U.S. soldiers were shot in war captivity. In May 1945 those responsible were sought after. Finally a U.S. military court charged 74 members of the I. *SS-Panzer-Division* "Leibstandarte Adolf Hitler" to have participated in this incident! As it is again currently known in Iraq, the accused were also then repeatedly psychologically and physically tortured (blackmail of confessions, mock executions, and similar). On July 16, 1946, the sentencing followed: without evidence, 43 death sentences, 22 life imprisonment, and 8 prison sentence lasting several years were declared! A wave of outrage followed that finally in 1948 led to the review of the sentences by a U.S. judge, as well as by three U.S. senators. The result was that in the USA the conduct of the case was declared as a "scandal" and "disgrace for the American flag." Subsequently all accused were released from custody.

The humming of the artillery was clearly heard despite the noise from the vehicles.
At a road fork a short pause; meeting of the Kommandanten *by the* Kompaniepanzer, *and then we continued at a faster pace, as well as we could in this darkness. We passed road signs, but could not understand what was on them.*
Our tanks left the street and drove across country into a section of forest in which we later briefly encountered a Kompanie Panzergrenadiere *that were preparing for attack. As welcome reinforcement we were to participate from then on in the ranks of this unit in the three-day fighting for the twin villages Krinkelt - Rocherath.*
With the tanks, we broke into the town. The Americans had brought Pak and Scherman-Panzer into position. They dominated the streets and paths, and despite the darkness destroyed multiple Panther at the beginning of the attack. The American infantry had moved from the edge of town to the rear houses, and we established ourselves in evacuated houses. A larger building, presumably a boarding school, because a washing room was available, served the Grenadier-Bataillon *for three days as a command post, and the large basement served as an assembly area for those severely injured. Not until now did we learn with who we were on the northernmost sector of the Offensive: the* Grenadiere *belonged to the II./*SS-Panzer-Grenadier-Regiment *25 of the 12.* SS-Panzer-Division *"Hitlerjugend."*
After a three-day uninterrupted battle for Krinkelt, in which sections of the 277. Volks-Grenadier-Division *also participated, we finally pulled out toward Malmédy; beforehand we received entries from our hosts in our pay books for three close combat days."*

The reasons for the ill success of the first days of attack were primarily due to heavy resistance from the U.S. troops, who were outstandingly supported by heavy artillery. Furthermore, the numerous American and even German mine fields, and the fact that the tanks and other vehicles could only drive on a few streets due to the weather conditions (muddy, sodden ground). Because all units moved into this area, there was consistent congestion—not least due to the frequently inexperienced driver. The quick advance that Hitler planned was also impossible. Thus, the Ardennes Offensive failed on the first day. The *Kommando* mission of the *Panzer-Brigade* 150 to reach the bridges before the hypothetical U.S. troops "pouring back" was unnecessary.

Because the LXVII. *Armee-Korps* did not succeed in conquering the strategically important Elsenborn—military training area that prevented any heavy U.S. artillery advance—the single actual success of the 6. *Panzer-Armee* was the SS-*Panzergruppe* "Peiper," that on December 18, 1944—after heavy combat by Stavelot—reached La Gleize. While *SS-Obersturmbannführer* Peiper attempted to keep the attack going over

Stoumont and Chevron, the U.S. reserves, led posthaste from other front sectors, cut off the breakthrough area by Stavelot. During the heavy fighting, only sections of the following German *Kampfgruppen* of the I. *SS-Panzer-Division* succeeded in closing the ranks to the *SS-Panzergruppe* "Peiper." In the meantime, they not only suffered from lack of fuel and munitions, but also of infantry forces in securing the armored vehicles. These were largely destroyed—simply with bazookas, among other things. When the opponent succeeded in finally closing the front by Stavelot, the *SS-Panzergruppe* "Peiper" was encircled in the Stoumont - La Gleize region.

The failure of the Ardennes Offensive within the framework of the 6. *Panzer-Armee* led to the invalidity of Operation "Greif." While *Kampfgruppe* "X" was not further utilized in the rear territory north of Losheimergaben, *Kampfgruppe* "Y" transferred to Engelsdorf (Ligneuville). *Kampfgruppe* "Z," which was led by *SS-Hauptsturmführer* von Foelkersam[37] since December 16, 1944, initially advanced on December 18, 1944, from the assembly area into the area south of Büllingen. From here it was to follow the *SS-Kampfgruppe* "Hansen" (reinforced *SS-Panzer-Grenadier-Regiment* 2), occupy the Maas bridge by Huy, and on December 20, 1944, set out to *Kampfgruppe* "Y" to Engelsdorf. The *Panzer-Brigade* 150 was to attack to the north from here, occupy Malmédy and, in doing so, establish the connection to the encircled *SS-Panzergruppe* "Peiper" to the west.

In the following assignment it became apparent that *SS-Obersturmbannführer* Skorzeny was not only unfit for such a classic attack, but also did not possess any sense of responsibility for his soldiers. Without prior reconnaissance and assembly of his forces, he ordered the *Kampfgruppe* "Y" on the evening of December 20, 1940, to attack Malmédy over Baugnez. During the attack—at minus 15 degrees—there was consistent heavy resistance fire and heavy losses, whereby *Hauptmann* Scherf ordered the return to the initial position of Engelsdorf. The *SS-Fallschirmjäger* and *Grenadiere* of the *SS-Jagdverband* "Mitte" (*Kampfgruppe* "Z") attacked separately at 0430 hours on December 21, 1944, over Bellevaux - Falize. They were to occupy Warchebrück and advance from the west toward Malmédy. The operation failed, after which the men triggered numerous flares with trip wire that were laid by the Americans, and thereby attracted artillery fire. Approximately two hours later the attack was repeated with five altered Panzer V "Panther," as well as a *Beutepanzer* "Sherman" of the *Panzer-Kompanie* "Dreier." *SS-Hauptsturmführer* von Foelkersam ordered three tanks to support the *Grenadiere* and *Fallschirmjäger* toward Warchebrück and three tanks to drive a relief attack from Falize toward Malmédy. The deployed tanks were brought down within a short time. This altered Panzer V brought a

---

37 *SS-Obersturmbannführer* Hardieck was fatally wounded on December 16, 1944, on a reconnaissance trip.

wounded *Offizier* to the command post of the *Kampfgruppe* "Z"—the restaurant "Café du Rocher de Falize." Due to the high losses this attack was also discontinued. The units of the *Panzer-Brigade* 150 in the region of Bellevaus—leaning on the heights east of Falize—reinforced positions with a length of approximately 10 km. The left neighbor was sections of the *SS-Panzer Division* "Leibstandarte Adolf Hitler," while the right neighbor was sections of the 3. *Fallschirmjäger-Division*.

The losses of the preceding battles, which amounted to 50%, little affected *SS-Obersturmbannführer* Skorzeny. He expressed to the *Führer* of the *Kampfgruppe* "Y" that "the pile is just right now." After Skorzeny was wounded in an artillery attack, *Oberstleutnant* Wulf took over command of the Brigade on December 26, 1944. Two days later sections of the 18. *Volks-Grenadier-Division* relieved the *Kampfgruppen* of the *Panzer-Brigade* 150 in the positions south of Malmédy. Commanded to Cologne-Wahn, at the beginning of January 1945 the disbanding of the brigade followed, and the men set off to their *Stammeinheiten*.

Assignment at Malmédy
December 20 – 28, 1944

© Michaelis-Verlag Berlin, September 2004

A former member recalls his mission with the *Panzer-Brigade* 150:

"In November 1944 a Kampfgruppe-*similar unit of 180 men under the command of* SS-Obersturmführer *Leifheit (mainly the first* Kompanie*) was pulled from the* Bataillon, *assembled, and moved off to the Grafenwöhr military training area for a special mission. Here we met formations of all branches of service; a person only attracted attention if he did not wear a Knight's Cross. But we quickly discovered that it was primarily units whose* Offiziere *and* Unteroffiziere *could speak English. An intensive repetition of our military skills began: we were trained especially for night missions, long marches in unknown territory, shooting at night, during the day, with flares and at light, and house-to-house combat.*

At the beginning of December 1944, camouflaged as a 'Christmas trees' train we drove to the west and unloaded in Wahn by Cologne. The advance and preparation for the Ardennes Offensive, which began on December 16, 1944, followed. We remained by Malmédy, were pulled out from this sector on January 1, 1945, and marched back to Wahn by Köln. After the end of the mission there was a special leave. Around January 28/29, 1945, we were all—with this I mean the remaining 30, 40 men and the entire fleet, reinforced by captured jeeps and armored reconnaissance vehicles—in our Neustrelitz barracks again and prepared for January 30, 1945."

Members of the *SS-Fallschirmjäger-Bataillon* with conferred
Fallschirmschützen insignia.

Identification tag of the *SS-Fallschirmjäger-Bataillon 600*.

Mission on the Oder Front

On January 12, 1945, the Soviet Winter Offensive began from multiple bridgeheads on both sides of Warsaw. The German formations had nothing to counter this onslaught. The *Heeresgruppe* "A" was just as annihilated as the *Heeresgruppe* "Mitte" within just a few days. On January 21, 1945, the *Heeresgruppe* "Weichsel" was quickly formed, which was to lead the front between Danzig - Stettin - Schlesien. The *Reichsführer-SS* Himmler was appointed to *Oberbefehlshaber* on January 26, 1945.

At the end of January 1945 sections of the Soviet I. *Weißrussische Front* (*Marschall* Shukow) had reached the Oder, and German formations in replenishment or in formation received the immediate transfer order to the front. Himmler supported his new *Heeresgruppe* "Weichsel" with numerous SS formations within just a few days. Among these were also sections of the *SS-Jägerverbände* that during action was under the control of the *Reichssicherheitshauptamt*.

The *Kommandeur* of the *SS-Jagdverbände*, *SS-Obersturmbannführer* Skorzeny received the order from the *Heeresgruppe* "Weichsel" on January 30, 1945, to march to Schwedt with all units immediately available and form a bridgehead position east of the Oder. On one hand this was to become the focused target of the German troops pouring back, and on the other hand represented a starting point for a German counteroffensive to be carried out short-term.

The head of the *Generalstab* of the army, *Generaloberst* Guderian—with the 6. (SS-)[38] *Panzer-Armee*, to be transferred from Ardennes to the east—was to advance from the region southeast of Stettin toward the south and unite with the German troops, who were approaching from the Guben - Glogau region. Through this, the entire Oder Front was to be relieved, and the advancing formations of the I. *Weißrussische Front* toward the west were to be annihilated. In doing so, the *Nord-* and *Südgruppe* each would have had to cover "only" roughly 70 km. During the simultaneous arrival of the *Sicherungsverbände* along the Oder, success was within the realms of possibility. Hitler refused, because he classified the relief of Budapest as more important. Rather, he commanded a solution, for which the newly formed 11. *Armee* under the command of *SS-Obergruppenführer* and *General der Waffen-SS* Steiner was to advance with the XXXIX. *Panzer-Korps* from the region between Madü-See and south of Stargard over Pyritz toward Schwedt. Not only were the encircled occupying troops freed from Pyritz successfully, but were also in contact with the advancing troops from the Schwedt bridgehead; the enemy west of the line was annihilated

---

38 The 6. *Panzer-Armee* was also identified as 6. *SS-Panzer-Armee* since January 1945.

and the front reduced. The distance between the troops of the XXXIX. *Panzer-Korps* and the Schwedt bridgehead amounted to roughly 70 kilometers.

After *SS-Obersturmbannführer* Skorzeny received the order for action, he immediately alerted the

> *SS-Fallschirmjäger-Bataillon* 600 (*SS-Hauptsturmführer* Milius)
> 4 *Kompanien*
> *SS-Jagdverband* "Mitte" (*SS-Hauptsturmführer* Fucker)
> 4 *Kompanien*
> *SS-Jagdverband* "Nordwest"[39] (*SS-Hauptsturmführer* Hoyer)
> 1. *Kompanie*
> *SS-Nachrichten-Kompanie*
> *SS-Scharfschützen-Zug*
> *SS-Infanterie-Geschütz-Kompanie*

and ordered the first *Vorkommando* march to Schwedt on the morning of January 31, 1945. Contrary to various reports the city—lying on the left Oder shore—was still not occupied by the Red Army, but rather was under the command of a badly injured *Oberst*. The troops in Schwedt were:

> *Panzer-Grenadier-Ersatz-Bataillon* 3
> *Panzer-Grenadier-Ersatz-Bataillon* 9
> *Panzer-Grenadier-Ersatz-Bataillon* 83
> *Pionier-Ersatz-Abteilung* 12
> *Fähnrichlehrgang* (180 men)

SS-Obersturmbannführer Skorzeny—appointed by the *Heeresgruppe* "Weichsel" as *Kampfkommandant* of the Schwedt bridgehead—immediately extended the defense positions by approximately 40 km in length. They initially ran in the north of Nipperwiese—which because of the Röhrike river practically constituted a small second bridgehead—toward west of Uchtdorf in the territory east of Grabow. Here by Königsberg an advanced position was developed. Finally, the HKL ran in a westward direction and ended between Peetzig and Niedersaaten on the Oder. While the *SS-Fallschirmjäger-Bataillon* moved into the southern sector—the 3. *Kompanie* was located in Königsberg—the *SS-Jagdverband* "Mitte" took over the northern sector position.

The Red Army was aware of the potential threat by the bridgehead, and in the first days of February 1945 attempted to repeatedly crush it in heavy attacks. While one endeavored on the German side to bring order to the *Alarmeinheiten* positioned on the Front, the *SS-*

---

39   Shortly afterwards this *Kompanie* was placed under the *SS-Jagdverband* "Mitte."

Jagdverbände fought off the strong Soviet tank attacks in heavy combat. On the evening of February 4, 1945, the opponent attacked the Bernikow combat outpost (east of Königsberg) with 30 T-34, infantry, and cavalry, overran the positions of the 3./*SS-Fallschirmjäger-Bataillon* 600 and penetrated into Königsberg with the majority of the tanks from the north and south. Although there was success in taking down nine enemy tanks with *Panzerfäuste* during street fighting, the town had to be cleared of the superior forces. The *Kompanieführer* (*SS-Obersturmführer* Marcus) succeeded in evacuating a number of civilians at the actual bridgehead position.

Mission at Schwedt Bridgehead

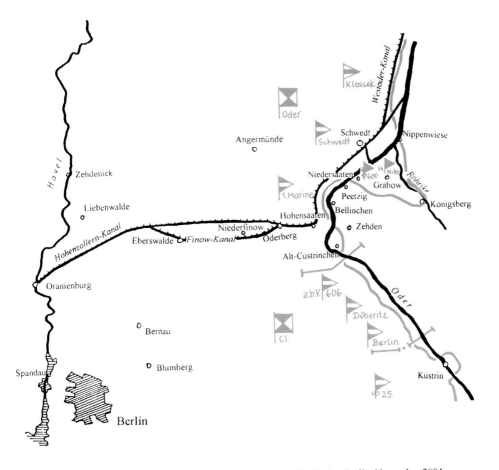

© Michaelis-Verlag Berlin, November 2004

On the same day the *Generalkommando* "Oderkorps" (*Generalleutnant* Krappe[40]) was formed from the *Stab* of the Division z. b. V. 612—a *Stab* in command of *Alarmeinheiten*—which was formed on January 26, 1945, in *Wehrkreis* X. Initially still under the command of the 11. *Armee*, the *Oderkorps* had at its disposal:

> *Kampfgruppe* "Klossek"[41]
> *SS-Kampfgruppe* "Skorzeny"
> I. *Marine-Schützen-Division*

While the SS-*Kampfgruppe* "Skorzeny" was located at the bridgehead, the *Kampfgruppe* "Klossek" constituted the left neighbor on the western shore of the Oder, and likewise the I. *Marine-Schützen-Division* on the western shore of the Oder—including the Zehden bridgehead—the right neighbor. For the defense Skorzeny received further supplied units; among others, the *Wachbataillon* "Hermann Göring," *Heimat-Flak-Abteilungen* from Berlin and Hamburg, also a *Volkssturmbataillon* from Hamburg and two *Kompanien* of the *Waffen-Grenadier-Regiment* of the SS (Romanian). In contrast—still stationed on the front—the III./*Fallschirm-Jäger-Regiment* 26[42] (9. *Fallschirmjäger-Division*) had withdrawn.

On February 8, 1945, *SS-Obersturmführer* Marcus received the order to conquer back the lost Königsberg. After strong enemy counterattacks the 3./*SS-Fallschirmjäger-Bataillon* 600 had to pull back again from the won town after a short period. In the afternoon of the next day the fighting strength amounted to still 30 men! On February 9, 1945—after heavy artillery preparation—the Red Army led no less than 12 attacks against the bridgehead position (sic!). On February 10, 1945, it amounted to three, and on February 12, 1945, to four attacks. Grabow, which was the decisive pillar in the defense of the bridgehead, was finally surrounded by *Panzerwracks*, which spoke of the hardship of the battles!

On February 16, 1945, along with the German Operation "Sonnenwende," planned in just several days the socalled Pomeranian Offensive began. While the III. (Germanic) *SS-Panzer-Korps* reached the encircled city Arnswalde, and was able to evacuate the 5,000 civilians and wounded, the XXXIX *Panzer-Korps* (*General der Panzertruppen* Decker) that were deployed to the west did not once succeed in advancing to Pyritz due to the heavy Soviet resistance.[43] On February 19, 1945, the *Heeresgruppe* "Weichsel" stopped the offensive "in order to avoid the worthless waste of the *Angriffsverbände*."

---

40   For the biography see Appendix 5
41   The *Kampfgruppe* "Klossek" consisted of:
        1 Hungarian *Bataillon*
        Grenadier-Regiment 1604
        Volkssturm-Bataillon Seesen
        1 *Bataillon Führeranwärter* of the *Generalkommando* "Oder"
42   The *Fallschirmjäger-Regiment* 26 was formed in February 1945 from the I. and II. *Bataillon* of the *Fallschirm-Jäger-Regiment* z. b. V., as well as the *Fallschirm-Panzerjagd-Bataillon* 52. The III./*Fallschirmjäger-Regiment* 26 was flown into Breslau and renamed *Fallschirm-Jäger-Bataillon* 68.

SS-Obersturmbannführer Skorzeny organized the *Ersatz-* and *Alarmeinheiten* supplied in the meantime to the bridgehead into a Division that was named Division "Schwedt":

Offiziere	*Unteroffiziere*	*Mannschaften*	*Stab*
	20	17	28
SS-Nachrichten-Kompanie	3	40	121
SS-Scharfschützen-Zug	1	-	40
Heavy *SS-Infanterie-Geschütze-Kp.*	1	32	120
Ausbildungs-Kompanie	2	8	150
Auffangkommando "Weiß"	1	6	160
Kraftwafen-Werkstattzug	4	17	74
Versorgungs-Kompanie	1	62	246
Sanitäts-Kompanie	11	-	65
SS-Fallschirmjäger-Bataillon 600	17	160	512
SS-Jagdverband "Mitte"	12	113	555
SS-Einheit "Schwerdt"	3	40	165
Bataillon "Aschenbach"	10	82	394
Bataillon "Jakobs"	17	174	672
Kompanie "Steinke"	1	37	83
Kompanie "Strassmann"	3	19	111
Bataillon "Strempel"	15	93	393
Bataillon "Zapf"	18	175	574
Kompanie "Galli"	1	8	45
Batterie "Klassen"	1	13	37
Pionier-Bataillon	17	117	514
Pionier-Sonderstab "Bernhardt"	7	28	27
	166	1,241	5,089

Deployed on the west bank:

Flak	25	134	626
Luftwaffe	5	30	250
W.-Gren.-Rgt. Of the SS (Romanian)	15	62	333
Volkssturm Hamburg	26	139	392
Volkssturm Königsberg	6	18	238
	243	1,624	6,928

43   Compare here: Michaelis, Rolf: *Die 10. SS-Panzer-Division "Frundsberg,"* Berlin 2004 and *Die 11. SS-Freiwilligen-Panzer-Grenadier-Division "Nordland,"* Berlin 2004

For a short time Skorzeny was able to have a *Sturmgeschützeinheit* that was actually considered for the Pomeranian Offensive: purely hypothetically, this unit was to stand by, if necessary, to push against the 10. *SS-Panzer-Division* "Frundsberg," advancing over Pyrits from the bridgehead. After a quick failure of the offensive this single maneuverable heavy unit—that at least engaged in several fights—pulled back from the bridgehead again.

After the failure of Operation "Sonnenwende" the *Oberbefehlshaber* of the *Heeresgruppe* "Weichsel," Himmler, pointed out the new tasks for the *Oderkorps* on February 22, 1945:

"Oder-Korps is to defend the Oder line and bridgeheads in its sector, with focus on the Schwedt bridgehead. The continued expansion and reinforcement of the defensive fortifications are especially important here with the broad formation of the troop. It must be checked and monitored daily. The weak artillery demands concentration and extremely flexible leadership. The necessary preparations for regrouping must be met in detail. If enemy conduct was also calm in front of the sector of the Korps until now, at any time it must be reckoned with a strong enemy attack (closing the ranks of the 47. Red Army). A surprising enemy advance against the deep flanks of the Schwedt bridgehead from the confusing Peetzig and Röcerbeck forests was obvious. To recognize this enemy intent on time must be the first objective of a running combat reconnaissance."

Five days later *SS-Obersturmbannführer* Skorzeny delivered the order to *SS-Obersturmbannführer* Kempin. It was determined to combine the *SS-Fallschirmjäger-Bataillon 600*, as well as the *SS-Jagdverband* "Mitte" into an *SS-Regiment*, and after the appropriation of two new *Bataillone* to use as *Reserve* at the bridgehead. Finally, they were to be pulled entirely from the bridgehead. From February 1 until February 25, 1945, both of these units had a total of 93 fallen soldiers, 294 wounded, and 5 missing (392 men = approximately 30% of the entire strength).

After the 2. *Weissrussische* Front (Marschall Rokossowkij) launched into the major offensive on March 1, 1945, from Madü-See over the Ihna to Nantikow, and within several hours brought nearly the entire front to a collapse, Hitler realized that no further offensive in the Pomeranian region would be possible. In order to spare men, he decided since the beginning of February 1945 to give up the highly competitive Schwedt bridgehead on the evening of March 1, 1945. Regarding this, the war journal of the OKW noted on March 2, 1945:

"The Schwedt bridgehead is no longer of any importance and has been vacated."

The number of fallen soldiers on the German side in the four-week battle amounted to approximately 400, and on the Soviet side approximately 1,000 men.

The former *Kommandeur* of the *SS-Fallschirmjäger*-Bataillon 600 recalls:

"We arrived at the bridgehead around February 1, 1945. Positions were located around Niederkränig/Grabow. Bataillon command post Hohenkränig. Reconnaissance was conducted as far as possible. Therefore, also the transfer of the 3. Kompanie under SS-Obersturmführer Marcus to Königsberg because we found the town to be clear of the enemy. The bridgehead was then expanded over Grabow, along the street Grabow – Königsberg. SS-Untersturmführer Gerullis, who blasted the church tower in Grabow that, among other things, was always under fire had mined everything in Grabow with his people, and such that the enemy will for days have had his 'joy' at the occupation of the town—after the explosion of the bridge over the Oder."

The hardship of the fights with the unbelievable numerical and material inferiority of the German defenders during the days from February 1 until March 1, 1945, led to numerous acts that were finally acknowledged with the conferment of the German Cross in Gold. Three soldiers—primarily for their mission at the Schwedt bridgehead—received these high decorations for bravery at the end of March 1945:

- *SS-Hauptsturmführer* Hunke as *Führer* of the *SS-Kampfgruppe* "Solar"
- *SS-Hauptsturmführer* Milius as *Führer* of the *SS-Fallschirmjäger-Bataillon* 600
- *SS-Obersturmführer* Marcus, as *Führer* of the 3./*SS-Fallschirmjäger-Bataillon* 600.

In the conferment recommendation for *SS-Hauptsturmführer* Hunke, *SS-Obersturmbannführer* Skorzeny described on February 20, 1945, the circumstances during the defense of the bridgehead in his capacity as *Führer* of the Division "Schwedt":

"Since February 3, 1945, Hunke has been the constant representative of the Divisionskommandeuer in the military command at the Schwedt bridgehead. It is in essence his duty that the bridgehead be maintained, expanded, and secured in its current form. Thereby, it must be considered that only two closed SS-Bataillone were at his disposal, while all other Bataillone were formed of soldiers of all sections of the Wehrmacht, that were caught from retreating "Splitter" and newly formed as quickly as possible, therefore initially had meager worth and morale for war. By untiring personal mission and his example, Hunke soon overcame all difficulties. He made a fundamental contribution to the formation and fortification of the Schwedt bridgehead. These facts must be recognized as leadership achievements of a special kind."

Positions on the Oder.

Zehden Bridgehead

After the *Heeresgruppe* "Weichsel," on February 27, 1945, organized the evacuation of the Schwedt bridgehead as soon as possible, the *SS-Fallschirmjäger-Bataillon*, in a strength of roughly 500 men, marched to Heinersdorf on March 2, 1945. Here the already planned merging with the *SS-Jagdverband* "Mitte" with the socalled *SS-Kampfgruppe* "Solar"[44] followed with the following organization:

Kommandeur:	*SS-Hauptsturmführer* Milius
I. *Btl.* (*SS-Fsch.Jg.Btl.* 600)	*SS-Obersturmführer* Leifheit
II. *Btl.* (*SS-Jagdverband* "Mitte")	*SS-Hauptsturmführer* Fucker
Heavy *SS-Infanteriegeschütz*-Kp.	*SS-Obersturmführer* Reiche
SS-Sturm-Kompanie	*SS-Obersturmführer* Schwerdt
SS-Nachrichten-Kompanie	*SS-Untersturmführer* Mussler
SS-Scharfschützen-Zug	*SS-Untersturmführer* Wilscher
SS-Versorgungs-Kompanie	

On March 5, 1945, the Division z. b. V. 610[45] took over the positions of the I. *Marine-Division* (*Generalmajor* Bleckwenn), which was actually to relieve the 9. *Fallschirmjäger-Division*. For this, the *SS-Kampfgruppe* "Solar" was placed under the command of the *Divisionskommandeur*, *Generalleutnant* Lendle.[46] They received the order to take over the Zehden bridgehead from the *Marineinfanteristen*. In a simultaneous attack on an exposed height in front of the bridgehead that served as the observation point for the Red Army, on March 6, 1945, the changeover of the bridgehead occupying forces took place. The then *Bataillonskommandeur* Milius recalls:

"The dividing line of both Bataillone *ran approximately from the Alt-Cüstrinchen train station over Hühnerpfühle - Grüneberg. My combat post was located east of the Oder between Alt-Cüstrinchen and the train station. The command posts of the* Fallschirmjäger *were in Alt-Cüstrinchen and Jagdverband 'Mitte' in Niederwutzen. The heavy* Infanterie-Geschütz-Kompanie *under* SS-Obersturmführer *Reiche, who was under our command, was a welcomed wonder. With the* SS-Fallschirmjäger-Bataillon *600 we had four* Fallschirmjäger-Geschütze *7.5 cm, and now six far-reaching 15cm* Infanterie-Geschütze. *We pulled two of these to the bridgehead, the remaining four remained in position west of the Oder.*

---

44 The name "Solar" was a code name from *SS-Obersturmbannführer* Skorzeny during the preparations of the Ardennes Offensive.
45 In addition the Division z. b. V. 610 led the:
I./*SS-Polizei-Regiment* 50
I./*SS-Polizei-Regiment* 8 (Hungary)
II./*SS-Polizei-Regiment* 8
10./*SS-Polizei-Regiment* 8
Volkssturm-Bataillon "Hamburg"
Volkssturm-Bataillon "Königsberg"
46 For the biography see Appendix 5

Furthermore, for antitanks we had three 7.5 cm Pak, Panzerfäuste, Panzerschreck, and later three Sturmgeschütze."

On the evening of March 6, 1945, Soviet artillery shells met an explosive charge fixed to the bridge over the Oder and destroyed it completely. Thus, the bridgehead was nearly cut off from the westward lines. Until March 24, 1945, it remained relatively calm by the bridgehead. The next day the Red Army took the offensive and transformed the four by four kilometer large bridgehead into a crater landscape through heavy barrage and bomb attacks. After an hour enemy tank and infantry forces arrived, during the course of which the *SS-Jagdverband* "Mitte" suffered high losses above all. On March 26, 1945, the opponent—after a two-hour bombardment—repeated the attack. Like on the previous

© Michaelis-Verlag Berlin, November 2004

day, the members of the *SS-Kampfgruppe* "Solar," also under high material and personnel losses, were able to fight off the attacker. When on the next day—the third major combat day in a row—the situation became unsustainable, *SS-Hauptsturmführer* Miluius ordered the mission of the bridgehead on the night before March 28, 1945, on his own authority. In doing so, he withdrew his from certain destruction—and came into a precarious situation: because he gave up the bridgehead position without superior orders, this could heave meant either the Knight's Cross or court martial proceedings. He received neither, but rather the promotion to *SS-Sturmbannführer*, as well as a written acknowledgement from the *Oberbefehlshaber* of the *Heeresgruppe* "Weichsel" on March 28, 1945:

"The Kampfgruppe *led by* SS-Sturmbannführer *Milius performed with great bravery at the Zehden bridgehead and carried out its assignment unwaveringly, as far as the conditions allowed. I express my special recognition to the brave* Führer *and men."*

The *SS-Kampfgruppe* "Solar" marched over Hohenwutzen to the Oderberg region for replenishment. Here at the beginning of April 1945 the previous I. *Bataillon*—the *SS-Jagdverband* "Mitte"—was taken from the formation, and ordered over Staaken to Deisendorf, in the *Alpenfestung* (alpine fortress). After the leadership attempted in the agony of the declining Reich to prevent signs of disintegration through draconian punishments, in resting position there was single drumhead court martial sentencing. A former member recalls:

"A comrade of ours was publicly hanged in Oderberg on the market square due to the report from an older woman concerning plundering. The sentencing was presumably declared by the court martial of the Korpsgruppe *'G' Angermünde. He had a small necklace, worth maybe 2 Reichsmark in his pocket...."*

Another member of the *SS-Fallschirmjäger-Bataillon* 600 likewise recalls a death sentence:

"In the vacated Oderberg, based on an absurd order, a young SS-Mann *who had arranged a couple of glasses of preserved strawberries was arrested by the* Feldpolizei, *sentenced by the special court, and hanged."*

Eberswalde Bridgehead

In February 1945 the Red Army could have presumably been in Berlin with the first tank formations. However, they halted at the Oder, and initially supplied the urgently needed supplies that began to decline due to the rapid advance since mid-January 1945. On the German side the time was used to establish the Oder front with positions and formations. Both succeeded poorly. The German Reich was at the end of any available resources. From—in the previous battles—beaten troops and untrained recruits, overhasty with *Volkssturm*, and convalescents formed *Alarmeinheiten*, nominal formations were formed, that mostly did not have any fighting strength. The organization of the *Heeresgruppe* "Weichsel" before the Soviet major offensive looked impressive only on paper:

> 3. *Panzer-Armee* with
>> *Verteidigungsbereich* "Swinemünde":
>>> *Seekommandant* "Swinemünde"
>>> Division z. b. V. 402
>>> 3. *Marine-Division*
>> XXXII. *Armee-Korps* with
>>> *Gruppe* "Ledebur"
>>> 549. *Volks-Grenadier-Division*
>>> 281 *Infanterie-Division*
>> *Oderkorps*:
>>> Division z. b. V. 610
>>> *Gruppe* "Wellmann"
>> XXXVI. *Panzer-Korps*:
>>> 547. *Volks-Grenadier-Division*[47]
>>> I. *Marine-Division*
> Available:
>> III. (Germanic) *SS-Panzer Korps*:
>> 11. *SS-Freiw.-Panzergrenadier-Division* "Nordland"
>> *K.Gr./23. SS-Freiw.-Panzergrenadier-Div.* "Nederland"
>> *SS-Kampfgruppe* "Solar"
>> *SS-Divisionsgruppe* "Müller"
>>> (sections of the 27./28.*SS-Freiw.-Grenadier-Division*)
>> 18. *Panzer-Grenadier-Division*
>> 4. *SS-Polizei-Panzer-Grenadier-Division*

---

47   In the 547. *Volks-Grenadier-Division* it dealt with, like with most formations, a quickly formed troop that consisted of the *Panzer-Grenadier-Regiment* "Oder" and the *Waffen-Grenadier-Regiment* of the SS (Romanian): Combat strength—practically nothing!

9. *Armee* with
 CI. *Armee-Korps*:
  5. *Jäger-Division*
  Divisionsstab 606 z. b. V.[48]
  Infanterie-Division "Berlin"[49]
 XI. *SS-Panzer-Korps*
  9. *Fallschirmjäger-Division*
  20. *Panzer-Grenadier-Division*
  Infanterie-Division "Döberitz"[50]
  169. *Infanterie-Division*
  712. *Infanterie-Division*[51]
 Festung Frankfurt[52]
 V. *SS-Freiwilligen-Gebirgs-Korps*
  286. *Infanterie-Division*[53]
  32. *SS-Freiw.-Grenadier-Division* "30. Januar"[54]
  Divisionsstab z. b. V. 391[55]
Available:
  25. *Panzergrenadier-Division*[56]
  Panzer-Division "Müncheberg"[57]
  Panzergrenadier-Division "Kurmark"[58]
  600. *Infanterie-Division* (Russian)

When on April 16, 1945, the already awaited Soviet major offensive began, the focus initially was in the area of the 9. *Armee*. The German formations, greatly inferior in number and equipment, could barely counter the onslaught. Until April 18, 1945, the I. *Weißrussische* Front succeeded in breaking through the German defense positions—above all the various *Korps* borders. The situation worsened so rapidly that both *Divisionen* of the III. (Germanic) *SS-Panzer-Korps* at the disposal of the 3. *Panzer-Armee* in the rear region were alerted, and commanded to the area of the LVI. *Panzer-Korps* respectively of the XI. *SS-Panzer-Korps*.[59]

---

48 Combat strength as per report on March 17, 1945: 4,460 men
49 Combat strength as per report on March 17, 1945: 5,889 men
50 Combat strength as per report on March 17, 1945: 3,474 men
51 Combat strength as per report on March 17, 1945: 3,699 men
52 Combat strength as per report on March 17, 1945: 9,039 men
53 Combat strength as per report on March 17, 1945: 3,266 men
54 Combat strength as per report on March 17, 1945: 2,846 men
55 Combat strength as per report on March 17, 1945: 3,618 men
56 Combat strength as per report on March 17, 1945: 5,196 men
57 Combat strength as per report on March 17, 1945: 2,867 men
58 Combat strength as per report on March 17, 1945: 2,375 men
59 Compare: Michaelis, Rolf: *Die 11.SS-Freiwilligen-Panzer-Grenadier-Division "Nordland,"* Berlin 2001

In order to reinforce the III. (Germanic) *SS-Panzer-Korps* again, the 4. *SS-Polizei-Panther-Grenadier-Division*—evacuated from Hela to Swinemünde on April 13, 1945, and assembled by Heringsdorf—received the transfer order to the Eberswalde region. The plans to merge the approximately 5,000 man strong Division with the new regiment-strong remainder of the 23. *SS-Freiwilligen-Panzer-Grenadier-Division* "Nederland" could not be carried out due to the events that arose very quickly.[60]

To intercept a foreseen Soviet breakthrough, the *Heeresgruppe* "Weichsel" assigned the *Kommandierender General des* III. (Germanic) *SS-Panzer-Korps*, *SS-Obergruppenführer* and *General der Waffen-SS* Steiner, to move into position at the joint between the 3. *Panzer-Armee* and 9. *Armee* between Liebenwalde and Oderberg. For this, the remainder of the 4. *SS-Polizei-Panzer-Grenadier-Division* was reorganized and renamed to *SS-Kampfgruppe* "Harzer." In addition to supplying numerous *Wehrmachteinheiten*, the *SS-Fallschirmjäger-Bataillon* 600 was also integrated into the new *Kampfgruppe*. In doing so, the *SS-Fallschirmjäger* formed the third Bataillon in the weak—reinforced by those delivered from the *SS-Feldersatz-Regiment* 13—*SS-Polizei-Panzer-Grenadier-Regiment* 7 (*SS-Obersturmbannführer* Prager.[61]

While the newly formed *SS-Polizei-Panzer-Grenadier-Regiment* 7 marched into the Eberswalde territory as the first *Truppenteil* of the *SS-Kampfgruppe* "Harzer," the Red Army succeeded in piercing through at the joint between the CI. *Armee-Korps* and LVI. *Panzer-Korps* toward Bernau. The troops of the CI. *Armee-Korps* (25. *Panzergrenadier-Division*, 5. *Jäger-Division*, SS-*Panzerjäger-Abteilung* 560, and *Sturmgeschütz-Brigade* 184[62]) were forced back north into the Eberswalde region, and moved into bridgehead position with the *SS-Polizei-Panzer-Grenadier-Regiment* 7 arriving south of the Finow canal, from where they were to again arrive toward the south to the LVI. *Panzer-Korps*; an order that could no longer be realized. The LVI. *Panzer-Korps* was already forced back to the Blumberg region—the opponent pushed far to the west by the break in the front. To conceal the lengthening south flank of the 3. *Panzer-Armee*, the *Heeresgruppe* "Weichsel" ordered the III. (Germanic) *SS-Panzerkorps* to the *Armeegruppe* "Steiner" to increase, and to move into the line Spandau - Oranienburg - Finowfurt on April 21, 1945. For this purpose the 3. *Marine-Division*, among others, was ordered from Wollin to Zehdenick. The *SS-Kampfgruppe* "Harzer," that was actually to follow the *SS-Polizei-Panzer-Grenadier-Regiment* 7 (with *SS-Fallschirmjäger-Bataillon* 600) into the Eberswalde bridgehead - CI. *Armee-Korps*, was likewise ordered to the Oranienburg region. With this the *SS-Kampfgruppe* "Harzer" was divided in the field.

---

60   The 23. *SS-Freiwilligen-Panzer-Grenadier-Division* "Nederland" then consisted only of the—located in the area west of Stettin in new formation—*SS-Freiwilligen-Panzer-Grenadier-Regiment* 48, a Bataillon of the *SS-Freiwilligen-Panzer-Grenadier-Regiment* 49, the *SS-Freiwilligen-Artillerie-Regiment* 54, as well as the remainder of further *Divisionstruppen*. The *Oberbefehlshaber* of the PzAOK 3, General *der Panzertruppe* von Manteuffel assessed the fighting value of the formation on March 26, 1945, with:
"The Division is practically only a reinforced Regimentstruppe*, infantry fighting power practically annihilated at the time, need for a completely new formation. The time of the end of replenishment not to be overlooked currently, therefore only for fit for defense, 'Kampfwert IV.'"*
61   Otto Prager was born in Plauen on December 3, 1912, and on December 9, 1944, as *SS-Sturmbannführer* and *Führer* of the *SS-Polizei-Panzer-Grenadier-Regiment* 7 was awarded the Knight's Cross of the Iron Cross. He fell presumably on April 29, 1945, during heavy combat in Neubrandenburg.
62   On April 7, 1945, the *Sturmgeschütz-Brigade* 184 reported an equipment of 23 *Sturmgeschützen* III and 8 *Sturm-Haubitzen* 42.

The quick advance of the enemy formations, as well as the German inferior forces, caused the German leadership to disregard the planned attack at the flanks of the Red Army. In order to spare forces and material, the CI. *Armee-Korps* was permitted to give up the Eberswalde bridgehead. On April 23/24, 1945, the units pulled back to the northern shore of the Hohenzollern Canal. The released forces—the 25. *Panzergrenadier-Division* as well as the *SS-Polizei-Panzer-Grenadier-Regiment 7*—were to be supplied immediately to the III. (Germanic) *SS-Panzer-Korps*, which was in Oranienburg, involved in heavy fighting. As was frequent, the facts superceded the orders. Due to the Soviet breakthrough through the "Randow-Stellung" in Mecklenburg-Western Pomerania, both troop formations received immediate marching orders to the XXXXVI. *Panzer-Korps*.

Mission in Eberswalde Bridgehead
April 18-24, 1945

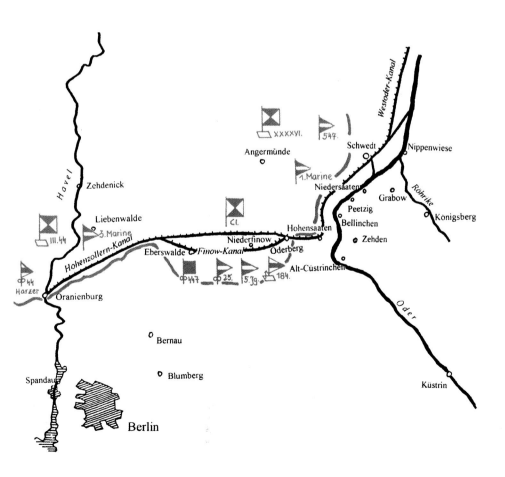

The Last Battles in Mecklenburg-Western Pomerania

As of April 20, 1945, the 2. Weißrussische Front with 49., 70., and 65. *Armee* south of Stettin had taken the offensive. Supported by heavy artillery and massive air attacks, the enemy formations superior in force succeeded in setting over the Oder and advancing to the west. The German formations of the XXXII. *Armee-Korps*, *Oderkorps*, and the XXXXVI. *Panzer-Korps* partially put up bitter resistance. Thus, the Red Army was able to advance only 20 km in five major combat days. Then, however, the organized defense and the cohesion disintegrated. The troops of the 2. *Weißrussische* Front could cross the socalled "Wotan Stellung" along the Randow-Bruch without serious resistance on April 25, 1945. In order to stabilize the front here, the 25. *Panzergrenadier-Division*, as well as the *SS-Polizei-Panzergrenadier-Regiment* 7 with the subordinate *SS-Fallschirmjäger-Bataillon* 600, received the immediate transfer order to the XXXVI. *Panzer-Korps*.

On April 26, 1945, the *SS-Polizei-Panzergrenadier-Regiment* 7 arrived as the first formation over Prenzlau for the isolation of the enemy breach in the line Grünow - Baumgarten. The *SS-Männer*, who were to defend Prenzlau with the remainder of the *SS-Kampfgruppe* "Langemarck,[63]" could hinder neither taking of the city on the next day, nor the further advance of the Red Army. The improvisationally formed 3. *Panzer-Armee* was annihilated. The troops of the *Korps* had only approximately 10% of their authorized strength! The *Oberbefehlshaber* of the 3. *Panzer-Armee*, *General der Panzertruppen* Manteuffel, vividly described the situation on April 27, 1945:

---

63   So fought, for example, the II./*SS-Freiwilligen-Grenadier-Regiment* 67, formed from the socalled *Jugendbataillon*, at the Prenzlau airport. Compare: Michaelis, Rolf: *Die Grenadier-Divisionen der Waffen-SS – Band II*, Erlangen 1955

"Complete disbanding of the Verbände *"Langemarck," "Wallonien," I.* Marine-Division, *and the entire* Flak-Abteilungen, *as far as they lost their weapons with or without fault. I saw such pictures like today not once in 1918. From the Divisionen "Langemarck" and I.* Marine-Division, *only the brave* Kommandeure *and several people as far as they commanded them with voice and heart...."*

Because it became clear to him that the socalled "Uecker-Stellung" could not be moved into for defense, on the same day Manteuffel ordered the occupation of the socalled "Feldberg Stellung." Here he intended to direct the defense into more orderly paths. The 25. *Panzergrenadier-Division*, advancing in the meantime, was to support this together with the 7. *Panzer-Division*, likewise commanded in the Neustrelitz area.

On April 28, 1945, the XXXXVI. *Panzer-Korps* moved into position between Strasburg and Lychen. From left to right stood the remainder of the:

> 281. *Infanterie-Division*
> *Kampfgruppe/28. SS-Freiwilligen-Grenadier-Division* "Wallonien"
> *SS-Pol.-Panzergrenadier-Regiment* 7 with *SS-Fallschirmjäger-Bataillon* 600
> *Panzerausbildungsverband* Ostsee
> I. *Marine-Division*
> *Kampfgruppe/27. SS-Freiwilligen-Grenadier-Division* "Langemarck"

on the front, interrupted by the lakes. When two Soviet *Panzer-Korps* breached between the lakes by Feldberg and Fürstenwerder on a Front expanse of approximately 3 kilometers, this "Feldberg-Stellung" was already again history.

In further disbanding, the remainder of the German formations marched further to the west. The XXXXVI. *Panzer-Korps* moved into the line from Neubrandenburg over the Tollensee until Neustrelitz on April 29, 1945. Reinforced by the 25. *Panzergrenadier-Division* and 7. *Panzer-Division*, the civilian population, as well as the annihilated troops, were to secure the path to the Elbe.

On the same day the Red Army succeeded in pushing into Neubrandenburg. Here stood the rest of the 281. *Infanterie-Division* (Oberst Schmid), as well as the *SS-Polizei-Panzer-Grenadier Regiment* 7 (including the *SS-Fallschirmjäger*) under the command of the annihilated *Divisionsstab z. b. V.* 610 (*Oberst* Fullriede). Since these battles *SS-Obersturmbannführer* Prager was considered missing; *SS-Sturmbannführer* Milius handed his *Bataillon* to *SS-Obersturmführer* Leifheit, and took over the rest of the *SS-Polizei-Panzergrenadier-Regiment* 7. While it came to the most difficult battles in Neubrandenburg,[64] as well as in Neustrelitz, and both towns could be conquered from the enemy, the *Heeresgruppe* "Weichsel" received an order from the head of the *Oberkommando* of the *Wehrmacht, Feldmarschall* Keitel, that was completely unrealistic:

"The task of the Heeresgruppe *Weichsel, while keeping a firm hold on the south and east front, is to hit and attack the enemy, who broke through toward Neubrandenburg, with all available forces."*

Aware of the senselessness of this order, however, superior *Kommandostellen* tried as much as possible to withdraw their troops from Soviet war captivity and lead them over the demarcation line toward the west. On April 30, 1945, the troops of the XXXXVI. *Panzer-Korps* (remainder of the 25. *Panzer-Grenadier-Division*, 281. *Infanterie-Division*, 7. *Panzer-Division*, and "Splitter" of the 27., 28., and 33. *SS-Division*, as well as the *SS-Polizei-Panzer-Grenadier-Regiment* 7) reached the line Malchin - Waren. Together with numerous refugee treks, the units pulled back on May 1, 1945, to Karow. On May 2, 1945, the remaining 180 SS-*Fallschirmjäger* under the command of *Kommandeur SS-*

Fallback through Mecklenburg-Western Pomerania

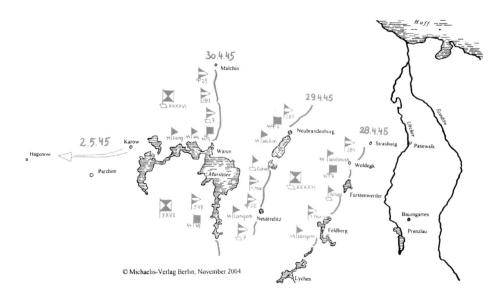

© Michaelis-Verlag Berlin, November 2004

---

64   Neubrandenburg was destroyed 80% by the battles!

Sturmbannführer Milius marched into U.S. war captivity. With this the *SS-Fallschirmjäger-Bataillon* 600 within the framework of the *SS-Polizei-Panzer-Grenadier-Regiment* 7 covered over 200 km from the first battles by Prenzlau on April 26, 1945, until May 2, 1945.

With this ends the one and a half years of war action for the *SS-Fallschirmjäger-Bataillon*. Although the partially mystical ideas of Himmler from December 1941—to form a "Verlorener Haufen"—no longer directly affected the formation of the *SS-Fallschirmjäger-Bataillon*, nevertheless, the first mission resembled that of a "Verlorener Haufen." The roughly 850 *SS-Fallschirmjäger* deployed had an approximately 650 man loss. Until the end of the war the *Bataillon*, which at formation had a strength of 1,140 men, could no longer be brought to an authorized strength. In the course of summer 1944, deployed as a "fire brigade" on threatened front sectors, the strength amounted always to only 200-300 men, because after the formation no further wave of *Bewährungsschützen* were pulled in. In fact, on October 1, 1944, the official end of the "Bewährungsformation" and the renaming of the unit to *SS-Fallschirmjäger-Bataillon* 600 followed. Reinforced by enlisted members of the *Wehrmacht*, in November 1944 the Bataillon had at their disposal 658 men and was ready for action. Subordinate to the *SS-Jagdverbände*, a partial assignment during the Ardennes Offensive followed, and finally extremely costly battles at three bridgeheads on the Oder against a superior enemy. The motivation of the *SS-Fallschirmjäger* led to a *Truppenteil* that contrasts with the majority of the German *Wehrmacht* and the *Waffen-SS*.

These roughly 180 paratrooper helmets found by Hagenow presumably came from the *SS-Fallschirmjäger-Bataillon* 600.

Appendix 1:
Chronology

09/06/43-12/00/43	Formation and infantry training in Chlum
12/00/43-03/18/44	Transfer to Mataruschka-Banja and paratrooper training in Kraljevo (Serbia)
03/28/44	Renaming to *SS-Fallschirmjäger-Bataillon 500*
03/19/44-04/05/44	Participation in Operation "Margarethe"
04/06/44-04/25/44	Quarters in Mataruschka-Banja by Kraljevo
04/26/44-05/10/44	Participation in Operation "*Maibaum*"
05/11/44-05/24/44	Quarters in Maturuschka-Banja by Kraljevo
05/25/44-06/10/44	Participation in Operation "*Rösselsprung*"
06/11/44-06/29/44	Refreshing in Laibach
06/30/44-07/04/44	Transfer to Gotenhafen
07/05/44-07/09/44	*OKW-Reserve* in Wesenberg/Estonia
07/11/44-09/15/44	Resistance combat in Lithuania
09/16/44-09/27/44	*Korpsreserve* in Schaulen
10/01/44 (m.W.v.)	Renaming to *SS-Fallschirmjäger 600*
09/28/44-10/00/44	Transfer by air transport to Vienna
10/15/44-10/00/44	Participation in Operation "*Panzerfaust*"
10/00/44-01/30/44	Refreshing in Neustrelitz
11/10/44 (m.W.v.)	Subordination to *SS-Jagdverbände*
11/00/44-01/15/45	Transfer of the *1. Kompanie* to Grafenwöhr for the formation of the *Panzer-Brigade 150* and participation in the Ardennes Offensive as of 12/16/44
02/01/45-03/02/45	Mission at Schwedt bridgehead
03/05/45-03/28/45	Mission at Zehden bridgehead
03/29/45-04/17/45	Refreshing in Oderberg area
04/18/45-04/25/45	Mission at Eberswalde bridgehead
04/26/45-05/01/45	Battle retreats at Prenzlau-Neubrandenburg
05/02/45	Imprisonment at Hagenow

Appendix 2:
Staffing and Military Post Service Numbers

Unfortunately, due to lacking documents, it is not possible to give a comprehensive staffing of the *Kompanieführer*. The names listed here reflect the ranks from Autumn 1944.

09/00/43-04/00/44	*SS-Sturmbannführer* Gilhofer
04/00/44-05/25/44	*SS-Hauptsturmführer* Rybka
05/00/44-04/26/45	*SS-Hauptsturmführer* Milius
04/27/45-05/02/45	*SS-Obersturmführer* Leifheit (m.d.F.b.)

1. *Kompanie*	*SS-Obersturmführer* Leifheit
2. *Kompanie*	*SiS-Obersturmführer* Scheu
3. *Kompanie*	*SS-Obersturmführer* Marcus
4. Kompanie	*SS-Obersturmführer* Droste

Military Postal Number 15 814	*SS-Fallschirmjäger-Bataillon*
Military Postal Number 28 933	*SS-Fallschirmjäger-Feldausbildungskompanie*

Appendix 3:
Uniforms and Equipment[65]

In December 1943 members of the *SS-Fallschirmjäger-Bataillon* received the special clothing for paratroopers for the first time at the *Fallschirmspringerschule* III in Kraljevo for jumping training (RZ 20parachute). These were worn until the end of the war, whereby the single modification was that after wear and tear no special paratrooper boots were given out. The fact is interesting that on the helmet, as well as the *"Knochensack"* (jump smock), the insignia of the *Luftwaffe* was kept.

The *SS-Männer*, along with their usual field blouse, which among the *Bewährungsschützen* did not display any rank insignia nor any SS collar patch, but rather two simple black patches, wore special field gray paratrooper pants. The pants, lined with drill or rayon, had two pockets and a fob in the front and two pockets in the back, one of which was for a first aid kit. All pockets had flaps—the front with press-studs, the back with plastic studs. At the knee on each exterior slits, each with three press studs, were

---

65 Compare here: Michaelis, Rolf: *Die Waffen-SS: Uniformen und Abzeichen*, Berlin 2001

worked in order to be able to remove the rubber knee bolster after landing. In addition, on the right pant leg a small pocket with two press-studs for the parachute jackknife were present. The bottom of the pants closed with ties, with which the pants could be worn in a socalled "draping over" above the shoes.

Over the field blouse the jump smock—1st style in gray or 2nd style in splitter camouflage—of the *Luftwaffe* (including the *Luftwaffe* eagle on the right breast side) was worn. This was made from drill fabric, and partially lined with beige cotton fabric or rayon. The jacket, which closed with a zipper, reached to the middle of the thighs, and was strapped around the legs for jumps and fixed there with press-studs. Both diagonal breast pockets, as well as both horizontal pockets at the waist were provided with zippers. On the backside there was an appliquéd pocket to the right for a flare gun, and to the left a loop for the handle of the folding shovel.

For the helmet, it concerned the paratrooper helmet model of the *Luftwaffe* from 1936. This was different from the normal *Wehrmacht* helmet due to the shortened, flanged visor edges. The sweatband had 12 round ventilation holes, and was fastened onto the steel helmet with a light metal ring and four socalled lentil head screws at six-millimeter diameter (one on each side and two in the back). Between the interior leather and the helmet were seven sponge pads used as possible shock absorbance. The gray-blue fastening straps made of goatskin, which could be secured with press studs, as well as metal buckles, separated in front of the ears so that each strap in front of and behind each ear provided a secure fit of the helmet.

The *SS-Fallschirmjäger* initially received the second style of the *Fallschirmschützen* boots of the *Luftwaffe*. These were higher than normal laced boots, were fastened with 12 metal inserts, and had mostly unstudded leather soles. After wear and tear the men received normal laced boots—sometimes the heavy mountain boots!

As was already mentioned, the men of the *SS-Fallschirmjäger-Bataillon* wore the special clothing of the *Luftwaffe* until the end of the war, without modification with the insignia of the *Waffen-SS*—sig runes on the helmet, or national eagle on the left upper arm. The jump smocks that repeatedly emerged in the last years in the socalled pea-pattern camouflage of the *Waffen-SS* leaves the question of originality open.

Appendix 4:
Fallschirmschützen Insignia of the Army

On September 1, 1937, the *Oberbefehlshaber* of the army, *Generaloberst* Freiherr von Fritsch, had introduced the *Fallschirmschützen* badge of the army for the members of the *Fallschirm-Infanterie-Bataillon* of the army. It could be presented to those who had completed six jumps. To continue to wear the achievement badge, at least six further parachute jumps had to be made each year.

The approximately 43 x 55 mm large badge that was worn on the left breast side displayed a gold colored wreath of oak leaves with the army eagle. On the wreath a silver colored eagle plummeting to the left was riveted. Until 1942 the *Fallschirmschützen* badge of the army was produced from light metal, and engraved on the back with the name of the recipient and the award number. As of 1942 the production followed in high-grade zinc.

Within the framework of the *SS-Fallschirmjäger-Batallon* after training at the *Fallschirmspringerschule* III, only those members who were not previously convicted were presented with the *Fallschirmschützen* badge. The *Bewährungsschützen* were also equally denied the conferment of the achievement badge, like the general reception with the decoration of bravery. With their court-martial sentencing the men were denied all conferred decorations up to now.

The *SS-Führungshauptamt-Inspektion Infanterie* conducted the conferment of approximately 200 *Fallschirmschützen* badges of the army to members of the *SS-Fallschirmjäger-Bataillon*.

Front and backside

Appendix 5:
Short Biographies

Eduard Aldrian was born on April 26, 1888, in Pola, and entered military service as *Fähnrich* on August 18, 1907. On November 1, 1911, he got his *Leutnant*'s commission in k. u. k. *Feldkanonen-Regiment* 8, and served after the First World War in the Austrian Armed Forces. Promoted to *Oberstleutnant* on April 1, 1936, he commanded the *Gebirgs-Beobachtungs-Abteilung* 38 as of August 1, 1938. On October 25, 1939, he took over— *Oberst* since August 1, 1939—the *Artillerie-Regiment* 619, and on November 9, 1941, the Arko 124. With the rank of a *Generalmajor* (since September 1, 1942), as of March 1, 1943, Aldrian led the Harko 308. Two months after his appointment to *Generalleutnant* on June 1, 1943, the command of the 373. *Infanterie-Division* (Croatian) was transferred to him. Finally, on January 20, 1945, the command of a Harko (306) followed once more. The General, honored with the German Cross in gold, died in Graz in 1955.

Fritz Fullried was born in 1895, and as *Oberstleutnant* and *Kommandeur* of the *Kampfgruppe* "Fullriede" in the 5. *Panzer-Armee* (*Heeresgruppe* "Afrika") he received the Knights Cross to the Iron Cross on April 11, 1943. From November 1943 until July 1944 Fullried commanded the *Fallschirm-Panzer-Grenadier-Regiment* 1 "Herrmann Göring." As the *Oberst* and *Kampfkommandant* of the Kolberg fortress he was presented the Oak leaves on March 23, 1945, as the 803rd soldier. Fullriede died on November 13, 1969.

Herbert Gilhofer was born in Linz on August 31, 1910, studied accounting, and entered the *SS-Totenkopf-Verbände* on January 7, 1935 (SS-Nr. 19 639). As of June 24, 1935, he was *Zugführer* in the *II./SS-Standarte* "Deutschland," and in 1938/39 followed the command of the 12. *SS-Reiterstandarte* in Schwerin as *SS-Obersturmführer*. Appointed to *SS-Hauptsturmführer* on March 1, 1940, Gilhofer arrived at the Front within the 1. *SS-Infanterie-Brigade*. Until summer 1942 Gilhofer was thereby honored with the War Merit Cross 2nd class with Swords and the Iron Cross II and Iron Cross I, as well as the East Front Medal and the Infantry Assault Badge. As a result of January 30, 1943, he received the promotion to *SS-Sturmbannführer*. From August 25 to September 25, 1943, Gilhofer participated in a course at the *SS-Panzer-Grenadier-Schule*, and afterwards was appointed head of the newly formed *SS-Fallschirmjäger-Bataillon*. On April 22, 1944, Gilhofer handed over the *Bataillon* to Rybka, and until May 16, 1944, belonged to the *Führerreserve* of the *SS-Führungshauptamt*. Then he commanded the 10. *SS-Panzer-Division* "Frundsberg." Here the *SS-Sturmbannführer* was awarded with the Close Combat Clasp 1st Class on October 26, 1944.

Nikolaus von Horthy was born in Kenderes (Hungary) on June 18, 1868. In 1886 he entered the k. u. k. *Kriegsmarine*, and in 1907 became first *Offizier* on a light cruiser. At the outbreak of the First World War he initially commanded an older admiral's ship, and in December 1914 took over the modern and fast warship "Novara." On March 1, 1920, von Horthy—meanwhile Admiral—was appointed to *Reichsverweser* of the Apostolical Kingdom of Hungary. On September 10, 1941, Hitler awarded him the Knight's Cross of the Iron Cross as *Oberbefehlshaber* of the Hungarian *Wehrmacht*. Because of his efforts for separate peace, on November 3, 1944, German troops arrested him. After the war von Horthy immigrated to Portugal, and died there in Estoril on February 9, 1957.

Günther Krappe was born in Schilde on April 13, 1893, and entered military service as *Fahnenjunker* on September 26, 1912. On March 12, 1914, he was appointed to *Leutnant* in the *Füsilier-Regiment* 34. After the First World War and assignment in the 100,00 Man Army, as *Oberstleutnant* (since August 1, 1936) he became (on October 1, 1937) *Kommandeur* of the *III./Infanterie-Regiment* 73. Appointed *Oberst* on April 1, 1939, at the outbreak of the war Krappe belonged to the *Gruppe* "Eberhardt" in Danzig. As of October 1, 1939, he was *Militär-Attaché* in Budapest, and as of May 1, 1941, in Madrid. In January 1943 Krappe—*Generalmajor* since November 1, 1942—participated in a *Divisionsführer* course, and from February 1, 1943, to December 15, 1944, led the 61. *Infanterie-Division*. Here, on October 1, 1943, he was promoted to *Generalleutnant*. In January 1945 followed a course for *Kommandierende General*, and at the beginning of February 1945 command of the *Oder-Korps*. A week later Krappe, honored with the Knight's Cross in April 1944, was assigned with the command of the X. *SS-Korps*.

Hubert Lendle was born in Schöntal on February 28, 1892, and entered military service as *Fahnenjunker* on July 24, 1911. On January 27, 1913, he got his commission as *Leutnant* in the *Infanterie-Regiment* 126. After the First World War and his time in the *Reichswehr*, as *Oberst* (since April 1, 1938) he commanded the *Panzerabwehrtruppe* V. In 1939 followed the taking over of the *Infanterie-Ersatz-Regiment* 26, and as of December 1, 1939, the command of the *Infanterie-Regiment* 345. At the end of 1940 Lendle commanded the *Infanterie-Regiment* 578 until March 31, 1942. After his appointment to *Generalmajor* on April 1, 1942, he commanded the *Sicherungs-Division* 221. In this official position he was promoted on June 1, 1943, to *Generalleutnant*. As of January 28, 1945, he led the *Divisionsstab* z. b. V. 610.

Dr. Alfred Leschinger was born in Böhmisch Tribau on May 2, 1906, and after his studies as a fully qualified lawyer served in the Czech army in the mid-30s. On January 1, 1937, he was appointed here to *Leutnant* of the *Reserve*. On January 30, 1940, Leschinger, with the rank of a *SS-Untersturmführer*, entered the *SS-Totenkopf-Infanterie-Ersatz-Bataillon*

II (SS-Nr. 351 360). The appointment to *SS-Obersturmführer* followed exactly one year later in the *SS-Totenkopf-Infanterie-Ersatz-Bataillon* I. From this unit the lawyer was transferred on April 15, 1942, to the *Nachschubkommandantur* of the *Waffen-SS* and *Polizei* "Russland-Süd." Here Dr. Leschinger received the rank of a *SS-Hauptsturmführer* of the *Reserve* on June 21, 1943, and on January 13, 1944, as *Gerichtsführer* the command of the *SS-Fallschirmjäger-Bataillon*. Dr. Leschinger was honored with the War Merit Cross 2nd Class.

Joachim Marcus was born in Berlin on November 14, 1920, and after his *Abitur* entered the 1. (E)/*SS-Standarte* "Der Führer" as *SS-Mann* on October 1, 1939, (SS-Nr. 311 760). On October 24, 1939, he was ordered to the 2./*SS-Standarte* "Der Führer." As *SS-Junker* he participated as of May 1, 1941, in the 5th course at the *SS-Junkerschule* "Braunschweig." After completion Marcus was appointed to *SS-Standarten-Oberjunker* on September 15, 1941, and transferred to the *SS-Division* "Reich." On January 30, 1942, he received the promotion document to *SS-Untersturmführer* and command of the *SS-Kradschützen-Ersatz-Bataillon*. From here Marcus was transferred on May 11, 1942, to the *SS-Panzer-Abteilung* 5. As of September 15, 1942, after being wounded, followed the assignment in the *SS-Panzer-Ersatz-Abteilung* in Weimar. One and a half years later—on May 15, 1944—Marcus was transferred to the *SS-Fallschirmjäger-Ausbildungs-Kompanie* in Kraljevo. On November 28, 1944, he took over the 3./*SS-Fallschirmjäger-Bataillon* 600. Marcus, honored with the Iron Cross II and Iron Cross I, as well as the Wounded Badge in Silver and the Tank Combat Badge in Silver, was presented with the German Cross in Gold on March 30, 1945.

Siegfried Milius was born in Warn/Müritz on June 10, 1919, and initially served with the *Polizei*; from October 1, 1933, until October 12, 1935, in the 4.(MG)/*Infanterie-Regiment* 6. On October 13, 1945, he joined the *SS-Standarte* "Germania," and was appointed here on March 12, 1938, to *SS-Untersturmführer*. On September 10, 1939, the promotion to *SS-Obersturmführer*, and on January 30, 1942, to *SS-Hauptsturmführer* followed. From July 27 until December 15, 1943, Milius was a member of the 3. *SS-Panzer-Division* "Totenkopf." After repeated wounds, as of December 15, 1943, he was in the *SS-Panzer-Grenadier-Ausbildungs-* and *Ersatz-Bataillon* 3. Because Milius reported to the *Panzerwaffe*, he participated from April 1 to 27, 1944, in a course at the *Schießschule* for *Panzertruppen* in Puttlitz, and from May 1 to June 3, 1944, at the *Panzertruppenschule* in Krampnitz. Surprisingly, on June 9, 1944, the command of the *SS-Fallschirmjäger-Bataillon* 500 followed. Milius, who already possessed the Wounded Badges in Black and Silver, both Iron Crosses, the Tank Combat Badge in Bronze, the War Merit Cross 2nd Class with Swords, and the Close Combat Clasp 1st Class, as well as the medal for March 13, 1938, and the Police Service Decoration, appointed to *SS-Sturmbannführer*—he was on

March 30, 1945, honored with the German Cross in Gold. The *Kommandierende General des Oderkorps, SS-Obergruppenführer*, and *General der Polizei* von dem Bach wrote in addition to this beforehand on March 9, 1945:

"SS-Hauptsturmführer *Milius is known to me as a bold* SS-Führer *inspirited with a very strong fighting will. During difficult resistance combat at the Schwedt bridgehead from February 1 to 13, 1945, Milius was the spirit of resistance in his sector against the opponent with superior powers that attacked again and again.*"

Benito Mussolini was born in Dovia di Predappio (Emilia Romagna) on July 29, 1883, and became a primary school teacher. In 1901 he joined the Socialist Party of Italy (PSI); however, one year later he left his home in order to evade military service. After being granted amnesty as a "deserter" Mussolini returned to Italy from Switzerland in 1905 and completed his military service. Initially a strict opponent of the war, in October 1914 he changed his stance and became a strong advocate of Italy's entry into the First World War. On August 31, 1915, Mussolini became a soldier, and in February 1917 reached the rank of an *Oberfeldwebel*. At the end of October 1922 King Victor Emanuel III appointed him *Ministerpräsident*. After the political and military failures of the years 1940-1943 the "Grand Council of Fascism" dismissed him on July 25, 1943—in addition to this Mussolini was arrested by order of Viktor Emanuels III. On September 12, 1943, German paratroopers freed him under the leadership of *SS-Hauptsturmführer* Skorzeny on the Gran Sasso (Abruzzo). Approximately 10 days later Mussolini formed a fascist rival government and proclaimed the "Socialist Republic of Italy." On April 27, 1945, Italian resistance fighters seized Mussolini at Lake Como during his attempt to flee to Germany and shot him the next day along with his mistress, Clara Petacci, in Giuliano di Mezzegra (Lake Como). Their disgraced bodies were hung publicly.

Alexander von Pfuhlstein was born in Danzig on December 17, 1899, and as *Fähnrich* entered military service on March 29, 1917. On December 14, 1917, he was hereby appointed *Leutnant* in the 4. *Garde-Regiment zu Fuß*. After his time in the *Reichswehr* he served as first *Generalstabsoffizier* in the 19. *Infanterie-Division* as of November 3, 1938. Thereby he reached the rank of an *Oberstleutnant* on June 1, 1939. He took over the same official position on March 15, 1940, in the 58. *Infanterie-Division*, and as of April 1, 1941, led the II./*Infanterie-Regiment* 18. From July 29, 1941, until March 2, 1942, it joined the command of the *Infanterie-Regiment* 77. *Oberst* since February 1, 1942, von Pfuhlstein led the *Infanterie-Regiment* 154 as of May 1, 1942. He commanded the Division "Brandenburg" from April 1, 1943, until April 10, 1944. Von Pfuhlstein, decorated with the Knight's Cross, resigned from active duty on September 14, 1944.

Kurt Rybka was born in Darmstadt on June 17, 1917, and chose the career of a *Führer* in the *Waffen-SS*. On May 1, 1940, he was appointed to *SS-Untersturmführer* in the *SS-Totenkopf-Kradschützen-Ersatz-Kompanie*, and from here was detached to *SS-Kampfgruppe* "Nord" on March 3, 1941. Wounded there, the transfer to the *SS-Kradschützen-Ersatz-Bataillon* followed, and from June 12, 1942 (*SS-Obersturmführer* since April 10, 1942), assignment once more in the *SS-Division* "Nord." As of April 22, 1944, Rybka—*SS-Hauptsturmführer* since January 30, 1944—took over the *SS-Fallschirmjäger-Bataillon* from *SS-Sturmbannführer* Gilhofer. Badly wounded during Operation "Rösselsprung," no further missions on the Front followed. In fact Rybka—honored with the Iron Cross II and Iron Cross I, as well as the Finnish Cross of Liberty 4th Class and the Wounded Badge in Black—led by *Ersatztruppenteil*: *SS-Panzer-Grenadier-Ausbildungs-* and *Ersatz-Bataillon* until the end of the war.

Otto Skorzeny was born in Vienna on June 12, 1908, and after his *Matura* studied mechanical engineering. In 1938 he joined the SS and served as of February 21, 1940, in the 2. (E)/ *Leibstandarte* of the SS "Adolf Hitler." In March 1940 the transfer to the *Ersatzsturmbann* of the *SS-Standarte* "Germania" followed. Having participated in the campaigns in the west as well as in the Balkans, on January 30, 1941, he was appointed to *SS-Untersturmführer*, and on April 20, 1941, to *SS-Obersturmführer*. After his assignment as *Regimentsingeniuer* in the *SS-Panzer-Regiment* 3, as *SS-Hauptsturmführer* in April 1943 followed the transfer as *Kommandeur* of the *SS-Sonderverband* Friedenthal z. b. V. On September 12, 1943, Skorzeny, with members of the 2./*Fallschirmjäger-Lehr-Bataillon* of the *Luftwaffe*, freed the arrested Mussolini on the Gran Sasso, and was thus awarded the Knight's Cross of the Iron Cross at the same time as being promoted to *SS-Sturmbannführer*. After Operation "*Panzerfaust*" in October 1944 Skorzeny was appointed to *SS-Obersturmbannführer*. He received a further special assignment relating to the Ardennes Offensive. Despite the failure and ill success of the *Panzer-Brigade* 150 during their mission on the Front, Hitler honored Skorzeny with the Honor Roll Clasp of the Army. For holding the Schwedt bridgehead he was awarded the 826th Oak leaves on April 9, 1945. Skorzeny, appointed to *SS-Standartenführer* of the *Reserve* on April 20, 1945, died on July 5, 1975, in Madrid.

Rainer Stahel was born in Bielefeld on January 15, 1892, and after his *Abitur* in 1911 joined the 1. Lothringische *Infanterie-Regiment Nr.* 130. As *Leutnant* he was *Zugführer* in the *Maschinen-gewehr-Kompanie*, and in 1916 was promoted to *Oberleutnant*. In the Royal Prussian *Jäger-Bataillon* 27, which consisted of Finish volunteers, Stahel likewise later led the *MG-Kompanie*. In 1918, as *Hauptmann* resigned from the Prussian military, he assumed Finnish citizenship, and as *Major* commanded the Finnish *Jäger-Regiment* 2. In the Finnish army followed the command of the 3. *Jäger-Brigade*, as well as command of the *Schutzkorps* in Abo as *Oberstleutnant*. In 1933 Kehl returned to Germany, and on February 23, 1934, assumed the position as *Hauptmann* of the *Luftwaffe* in the *Reichluftfahrtministerium*. As Major he served in 1938 with the light *Flak-Abteilung* 73. Promoted to *Oberstleutnant* in 1939, he led the *Reserve-Flak-Abteilung* 151. The command of the *Flak-Regiment* (mot.) 99 followed in 1943. Here, he was honored on January 18, 1942, with the Knight's Cross of the Iron Cross. One year later he was awarded the 169th Oak leaves, as well as promoted to *Generalmajor*. Transferred with the *Flak-Brigade* 22 to Southern Italy in summer 1943, Stahel was appointed *Stadtkommandant* of Rome. In 1944 he arrived again on the Eastern front and was initially *Kommandant* of the "Fester Platz" Wilna. On July 18, 1944, for this mission the promotion to *Generalleutnant* and the conferment of the 79th Swords followed. One week later Hitler appointed Stahel to *Wehrmachtkommandant* of Warsaw. The assignment as *Kommandant* of Bucharest followed, whereby the *Generalleutnant* was taken into Soviet war captivity in September 1944. He died on November 30, 1955, in Soviet custody shortly before his return to Germany.

Josip Broz Tito was born in Kumrovec (Croatia) on May 7, 1892, and as of 1907 completed his apprenticeship as a locksmith. In 1910 he moved to Zagreb and joined the Social Democratic Party of Croatia. As of 1913 he fulfilled his military service in the Austria-Hungarian Army, and in Zagreb *Heimwehr-Regiment*, with which he arrived at the Carpathian Front in January 1915, and in March 1915 came wounded into Russian war captivity. Released from captivity in 1917, he participated in Socialist demonstrations in Petrograd (now St. Petersburg) and joined the Red Guards. In 1920 Broz returned back to Zagreb and became a member of the newly founded Communist Party of Yugoslavia. After the ban on Communist activities in 1921 he initially worked as a mechanic in Veliko Trojstvo. In 1924 he became a member in the district committee of the (in the meantime) illegal Communists in Bjelovar. Four years later he was arrested as Secretary of the Provincial Committee of the KPJ in Croatia, and Broz served five years in jail. After his release Broz went underground, and was accepted in the *Zentralkomitee* (ZK) of the Exil-KPJ in Vienna. With his appointment in the Politburo he took the assumed name "Tito." In 1942 Tito opened the first meeting of the *Antifaschistischer Rat der Volksbefreiung Jugoslaviens* (Antifascist Council of the Volksbefreiung, AVNOJ), a delegated amalgamation of all groups involved in resistance. In November 1943, at the second meeting of the AVNOJ, the delegates chose him for president. At the same time he received the title *Marschall* of Yugoslavia. On March 8, 1945, Tito formed a new Yugoslavian government in agreement with the royal exile government, and on November 29, 1945, was declared *Ministerpräsident* of a federal republic. He died on May 4, 1980, in Ljubljana.

Rolf Wuthmann was born in Kassel on August 26, 1893, and entered military service as a *Fahnenjunker* on April 9, 1912. On November 10, 1913, he was appointed *Leutnant* in the *Feldartillerie-Regiment* 40. After his participation in the First World War and service in the 100,000 *Mann-Heer*, Wuthmann—*Oberstleutnant* since January 1, 1937—served as first *Generalstabsoffizier* in the *Gruppenkommando* VI. He held the same official position as *Oberst* (August 1, 1939) in the 4. *Armee*. On November 15, 1940, Wuthmann became head of the *Generalstab* of the 16. *Armee*. In this capacity he was promoted on February 1, 1942, to *Generalmajor*. From May 2 to November 16, 1942, he commanded the 295. *Infanterie-Division*. The official position of authorized General of Transportation, South Russia sector, followed. After the appointment to *Generalleutnant* on March 1, 1943, on April 2, 1943, Wuthmann became head of the transportation for ten weeks in the OKH. As of June 20, 1943, he commanded the 112. *Infanterie-Division*, and finally, as of December 5, 1943, the IX. *Armee-Korps*. Wuthmann was honored with the German Cross in Gold and the Knight's Cross.

Appendix 6:
Ranks: *Waffen-SS*/Army 1944

SS-Grenadier	*Grenadier*
SS-Sturmmann	*Gefreiter*
SS-Rottenführer	*Obergefreiter*
SS-Unterscharführer	*Unteroffizier*
SS-Scharführer	*Unterfeldwebel*
SS-Oberscharführer	*Feldwebel*
SS-Hauptscharführer	*Oberfeldwebel*
SS-Untersturmführer	*Leutnant*
SS-Obersturmführer	*Oberleutnant*
SS-Hauptsturmführer	*Hauptmann*
SS-Sturmbannführer	*Major*
SS-Obersturmbannführer	*Oberstleutnant*
SS-Standartenführer	*Oberst*
SS-Oberführer	no comparable rank
SS-Brigadeführer	*Generalmajor*
SS-Gruppenführer	*Generalleutnant*
SS-Obergruppenführer	*General*
SS-Oberstgruppenführer	*Generaloberst*

Index of Names

Sources and Literature

Bundesarchiv/Militärarchiv Freiburg

RH 19-II   RH 20-4

RH 21-3

RH 24-9/58   N 756/279

Bundesarchiv Berlin/ehem. BDC

SSO 003 C   SSO 013 A

SSO 032 A

SSO 037 B   SSO 064

SSO 057 B

SSO 063 B   SSO 068 A

SSO 075 B

SSO 088 B   SSO 098 A

SSO 109

SSO 122 A   SSO 164

SSO 208 B

SSO 252   SSO 257 A

SSO 296 A

SO 297 A   SSO 319 A

Dickert, Großmann: *Der Kampf um Ostpreussen*, Stuttgart 1985

Haupt, Werner: *Heeresgruppe "Mitte,"* Dorheim, 1968

Haupt, Werner: *Heeresgruppe "Nord,"* Bad Nauheim 1966

Keilig, Wolf: *Die Generale des Heeres*, Friedberg 1983

Kunzmann, Milius: *Fallschirmjäger der Waffen-SS im Bild*, Coburg 1998

Michaelis, Rolf: *Die Grenadier-Divisionen der Waffen-SS, Band II*, Erlangen 1995

Michaelis, Rolf: *Die Gebirgs-Divisionen der Waffen-SS*, Berlin 1998

Michaelis Rolf: *Die Panzer-Grenadier-Divisionen der Waffen*, Berlin 1998

Neubacher, Hermann: *Sonderauftrag Südost*, Göttingen 1956

Potente, Hilmar, u.a.: *Der Weg der 163. Infanterie-Division*, Berlin 1998

Preradovich von, Nikolaus: *Die Generale der Waffen-SS*, Berg 1985

Schramm, Percy (Hrsg): *Kriegstagebuch des OKW*, Herrsching 1982

Skorzeny, Otto: *Lebe gefährlich*, Siegburg-Niederpleis 1962

Skorzeny, Otto: *Wir kämpften – wir verloren*, Siegburg-Niederpleis 1962

Tiecke, Wilhelm: *Das Ende zwischen Oder und Elbe*, Stuttgart, 1994

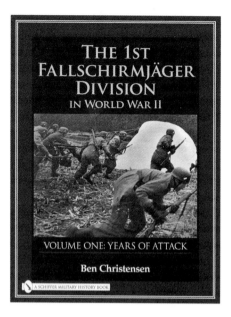

The 1st Fallschirmjäger Division in World War II
Volume One: Years of Attack
Ben Christensen

Based on their combat achievements, friends and foes alike have singled out the men from the German 1st Parachute Division as the best soldiers in World War II, as they at Eben Emael executed the most successful commando raid of the war; on Crete the most audacious attack; and in Monte Cassino the most dogged defense. A total of 129 Knight's Crosses were awarded to men from this division - twice as many as any other German division. For the first time a comprehensive book has been written about the fate of this division based on all available sources and with the invaluable aide of veterans from the division. It is a warts-and-all tale, which gives a candid insight not only to the battles from the German perspective, but also to the minds of the men who became the backbone of the division. The books contains more than 500 color and black and white photos, many of which have never been printed before. Furthermore, there are thirty unique maps in color, thirty detailed Orders of Battle, 500 short biographies of the key personnel in the division, and a list of all the division's Knight's Cross and the German Cross in Gold winners.

The first volume, Years of Attack, follows the recruitment and training of the Fallschirmjägers and their revolutionary vertical deployment in Scandinavia, Holland, Eben Emael, Corinth and Crete through to two tough tours as elite infantry on the Eastern Front. The second volume, Years of Retreat, follows the division from the battles of El Alamein, Tunisia, Sicily, Monte Cassino, Bologna, Normandy and Brittany to the final chaotic days before the capitulation. The battles are brought to life through nearly 1,000 eyewitness accounts and add new information to all the battles fought by elements of the German 1st Fallschirmjäger Division.

ISBN: 9780764327926   9"x12"   over 250 color/bw images   288 pp
Hard Cover $79.95

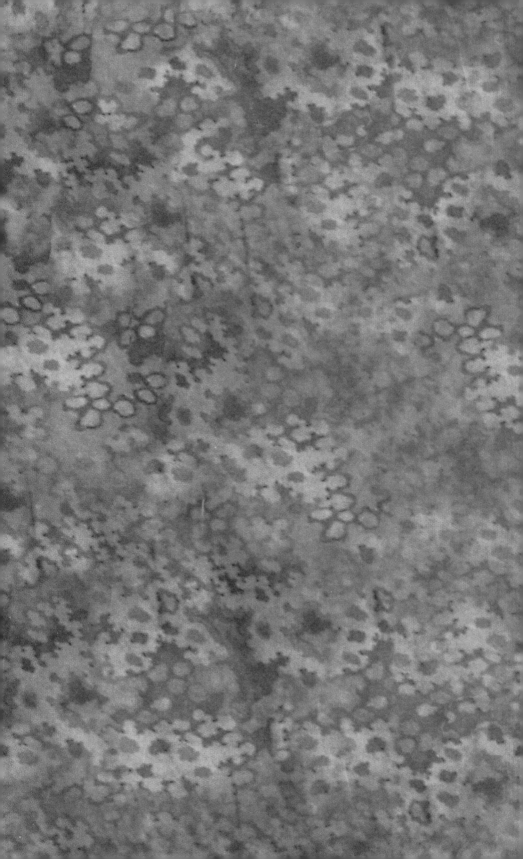